THE 4 STAGES OF PSYCHOLOGICAL SAFETY

Timothy R. Clark

THE 4 STAGES OF PSYCHOLOGICAL SAFETY

Defining the Path
to **Inclusion** and **Innovation**

Berrett–Koehler Publishers, Inc.

Berrett-Koehler Publishers, Inc.
1333 Broadway, Suite 1000
Oakland, CA 94612-1921
Tel: (510) 817-2277
Fax: (510) 817-2278
www.bkconnection.com

ORDERING INFORMATION
Quantity sales. Special discounts are available on quantity purchases by corporations, associations, and others. For details, contact the "Special Sales Department" at the Berrett-Koehler address above.
Individual sales. Berrett-Koehler publications are available through most bookstores. They can also be ordered directly from Berrett-Koehler: Tel: (800) 929-2929; Fax: (802) 864-7626; www.bkconnection.com.
Orders for college textbook / course adoption use. Please contact Berrett-Koehler: Tel: (800) 929-2929; Fax: (802) 864-7626.

Distributed to the U.S. trade and internationally by Penguin Random House Publisher Services.

Printed in the United States of America

Berrett-Koehler books are printed on long-lasting acid-free paper. When it is available, we choose paper that has been manufactured by environmentally responsible processes. These may include using trees grown in sustainable forests, incorporating recycled paper, minimizing chlorine in bleaching, or recycling the energy produced at the paper mill.

Library of Congress Cataloging-in-Publication Data

Names: Clark, Timothy R., 1964- author.
Title: The 4 stages of psychological safety : defining the path to
  inclusion and innovation / Timothy R. Clark.
Other titles: Four stages of psychological safety
Description: First edition. | Oakland, CA : Berrett-Koehler Publishers, Inc.,
  [2020] | Includes bibliographical references and index.
Identifiers: LCCN 2019033095 | ISBN 9781523087686 (paperback ; alk. paper)
  | ISBN 9781523087693 (adobe pdf) | ISBN 9781523087709 (epub)
Subjects: LCSH: Leadership. | Organizational behavior--Psychological
  aspects. | Corporate culture--Psychological aspects. | Employee morale.
Classification: LCC HD57.7 .C5376 2020 | DDC 658.3/82—dc23
LC record available at https://lccn.loc.gov/2019033095

First Edition

28 27 26 25 24 23 22 21   10 9 8 7 6 5 4

Cover designer: Travis Wu and Kirk DouPonce   *Author photo credit:* Chelsie Starley
Book producer and text designer: Leigh McLellan Design
Copyeditor: Karen Seriguchi   *Indexer:* Ken DellaPenta

To Tracey

Contents

Preface ix

Introduction 1

Stage 1 Inclusion Safety 19

Stage 2 Learner Safety 41

Stage 3 Contributor Safety 65

Stage 4 Challenger Safety 95

Conclusion Avoiding Paternalism and Exploitation 125

Notes 141

Acknowledgments 151

Index 153

About the Author 161

Preface

This book puts forward a theory of human interaction. Let me give you the context. Several years ago, my wife, Tracey, and I returned to the United States from England as I neared the completion of a PhD in social science at Oxford University. The ramen budget was gone. I would get a job, work for a year, finish my dissertation, teach at a university, and live happily ever after. That was the plan.

Here's what actually happened. I stepped out of the ivory tower into the gritty, sweaty megaton realm of a steel plant. Constructed by US Steel Corporation during World War II, Geneva Steel was the last fully integrated steel mill west of the Mississippi River, a hulking mass of machinery spread across 1,700 acres, the industrial equivalent of the Vatican, a self-contained enclave within a larger metropolis, with its own trains, fire station, hospital, and towering blast furnace cathedral. The plant manufactured steel plate, sheet, and pipe used to make everything from bridges to bulldozers. With my working-class sympathies, I thought I knew what I was getting into. I didn't have a clue.[1]

> **Key questions:** Have you ever been dropped into a completely foreign environment? Were you suspicious of the natives? What bias or prejudice did you bring?

This was another world. I found myself working with shift-work-hardened, layoff-endured welders, millwrights, pipefitters, and crane operators. These shadows under the hardhats became my friends, but there was nothing romantic about this heaving, grinding, snorting place. The shop floor was a high-stakes, no-margin-for-error arena where precision mattered and assumptions could kill. With thousands of safe-job procedures to govern every task for every job in every operation, nothing was left to chance. They preached safety so incessantly, it was easy to stop believing.

Then came the fateful day. A maintenance worker was crushed under a sixteen-ton load of iron ore pellets. He died instantly. I remember wondering what agony would sweep through the man's family. Later that day, I was given the assignment to accompany the CEO to deliver the dreadful news. We learned later that this tragedy was the result of several employees breaking safety rules. In the days ahead, safety would become my obsession, but not in the way you might think. I would come to learn that psychological safety is the foundation of inclusion and team performance and the key to creating an innovative culture.

With my degree in hand, it was time to leave the mill and trade my hardhat and steel-toed boots for tweed, chalk, and the classroom. Then something unexpected happened. The CEO asked me to become the plant manager. Now I faced an unusual decision: Settle into the tranquil life of an academic or lead a team of 2,500 employees working in the bowels of an industrial beast. Tracey and I decided to accept the offer. Why? Because it represented a rare opportunity to study human behavior in a unique setting as a participant observer. The experience would thrust me into a real-world tutorial and challenge the elegant theory I had learned at Oxford.

On my first day as plant manager, I called to order the morning operating meeting and came face to face with the indigenous culture. A stoic silence fell over the room as I peered into the faces of twenty superintendents, many of whom were old enough to be my father. Now they reported to me.

They had been deeply socialized to self-censor, constrained by deference to positional power and a slavish adherence to the chain of command. Power mattered. And these men (and they were all men) understood where power lay. It lay with me. Despite my youth and inexperience, they would render obedience to that source of power. Indeed, I was now the command center, the control tower, the alpha male. I had what the sociologist C. Wright Mills called "the most of what there is to have."[2] Experience had taught these managers that it was emotionally, politically, socially, and economically expensive to say what they really thought, so they smiled and nodded politely.

Key questions: Have you ever been in a position of power? Have you ever been in a position of no power? Did having power or not having power change your behavior?

Inhabiting this fertile setting for field study was a social scientist's dream. What I was observing cried out for interpretation. But I had to be more than an observer; I had to be a reformer. To improve the company's performance, we needed a transformation. The tired old plant was struggling to compete with the mini-mills that had disrupted the industry and were dominating the market. To increase throughput and yield, we needed to vacate the rules of naked force and disabuse people of their worship of coercive authority and their inclination to induce fear through intimidation. The entire organization needed to be cleansed from its status-bound model of authoritarian rule. Defang the place or die in the next downturn.

Commercial organizations survive by maintaining competitive advantage, which ultimately means incubating innovation. If you watch closely, you will notice that innovation is almost always a collaborative process and almost never a lightbulb moment of lone genius. As the historian Robert Conquest once said, "What is easy to understand may have not been easy to think of."[3] Innovation is never easy to think of. It requires creative abrasion and constructive dissent—processes that rely on high *intellectual* friction and low *social* friction.[4]

Most leaders don't comprehend that managing these two categories of friction to create an ecosystem of brave collaboration is at the heart of leadership as an applied discipline. It is perhaps the supreme

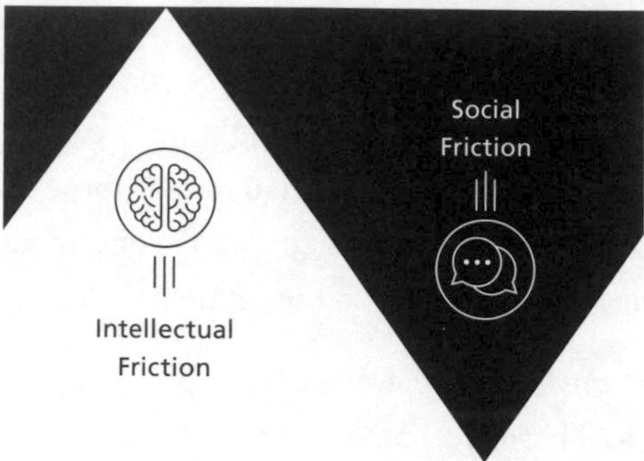

Figure 1. Increasing intellectual friction, decreasing social friction

test of a leader and a direct reflection of personal character. (figure 1) Without skill, integrity, and respect for people, it doesn't happen. Nor can perks such as foosball tables, free lunch, an open office environment, and the aesthetic of a hip organization bring it to life.

> **Key Concept:** The leader's task is to simultaneously increase intellectual friction and decrease social friction.

I was witnessing the opposite pattern, reflected in the absence of what we call *psychological safety*. I soon realized that my stewardship meant protecting people not only physically but also psychologically. As I learned firsthand, the absence of physical safety can bring injury or death, but the absence of psychological safety can inflict devastating emotional wounds, neutralize performance, paralyze potential, and crater an individual's sense of self-worth. The implication is that organizations that lack psychological safety and compete in highly dynamic markets are galloping their way to extinction.

One of the first things you learn about leadership is that the social and cultural context has a profound influence on the way people behave and that you as the leader are, straight up, responsible for that context. The other thing you learn is that fear is the enemy. It freezes initiative, ties up creativity, yields compliance instead of commitment, and represses what would otherwise be an explosion of innovation.

Key principle: The presence of fear in an organization is the first sign of weak leadership.

If you can banish fear, install true performance-based accountability, and create a nurturing environment that allows people to be vulnerable as they learn and grow, they will perform beyond your expectations and theirs.

Key questions: Have you ever been a part of an organization that was dominated by fear? How did you respond? How did other people respond?

My informal ethnographic analysis as plant manager at Geneva Steel lasted five years. That defining experience set me on a path to understand why some organizations unleash the potential of individuals and other can't. For the past twenty-five years, I've been a working cultural anthropologist and a student of psychological safety, learning from leaders and teams across every sector of society.

I've discovered that psychological safety follows a progression based on the natural sequence of human needs. (figure 2) First, human beings want to be included. Second, they want to learn. Third, they

Figure 2. The 4 stages of psychological safety

want to contribute. And finally, they want to challenge the status quo when they believe things need to change. This pattern is consistent across all organizations and social units.

> **Key concept:** Psychological safety is a condition in which you feel (1) included, (2) safe to learn, (3) safe to contribute, and (4) safe to challenge the status quo—all without fear of being embarrassed, marginalized, or punished in some way.

All human beings have the same innate need: We long to belong. As a homeless man wrote on a tattered piece of cardboard, "Be kind if you're not my kind." Not long ago, my sardonic teenage daughter, Mary, went to a high school basketball game and held up a poster that revealed a penetrating truth: "I'm just here so I don't lose friends!" Though we long to belong, we see broken human interaction everywhere we look.

This book addresses broken human interaction. I'm writing primarily to business leaders, but my message applies to any social unit. I want to shine a light on how we get along, decode the science of silence, and explore what it takes to liberate our voices and connect more effectively. Specifically, I want to share with you what I've learned about the way psychological safety influences behavior, performance, and happiness. What's the mechanism? How do we activate or deactivate it?

I'm in the pattern-recognition business. When it comes to the way people interact, the patterns are unmistakable, and the challenge is universal. What I have to say is both empirical and normative. I make no apologies for combining cold, dispassionate observations with warm, passionate pleas because the use case, the job to be done, is to offer practical guidance. I'll share examples from work life, school, and home, drawing heavily on my own experience because what I have learned at home mirrors what I've learned in organizations.

> **Key question:** Have you ever had the realization that family life is almost always the most challenging place to model and apply correct principles of human interaction?

Sometimes we're noble and good to each other. Sometimes we're criminally irresponsible. Our track record as a species is, for the most part, a chilling history, a pageant of war, and a chronicle of conquest. Maya Angelou rendered the lamentable past as few literary voices can: "Throughout our nervous history, we have constructed pyramidic towers of evil, ofttimes in the name of good. Our greed, fear and lasciviousness have enabled us to murder our poets, who are ourselves, to castigate our priests, who are ourselves. The lists of our subversions of the good stretch from before recorded history to this moment."[5]

Why, after thousands of years, are we technologically advanced and still sociologically primitive?

As social creatures, we act like free electrons, demonstrating both connection and contention. It's true that we need each other to flourish. Yet despite knowing this, we suffer from compassion fatigue, are handicapped by our blind spots, and chronically regress to the mean. We go through cycles of embracing and exiling each other. Indeed, the study of humans in social settings is largely the study of exclusion and fear. For example, a mere third of US workers believe their opinions count.[6]

Key questions: Do you feel included and listened to at work? How about school? How about home?

Despite our unique life stories, we share common experiences. We have all felt the pain of rejection and reproach. At the same time, we've all done some excluding and segregating, some manipulating and controlling, some depriving and belittling, some friending and unfriending. We've all drawn racial, social, or other demographic or psychographic lines, and made unjust judgments on others and treated them poorly. We know something about marginality because we've all been marginalized. We can be benevolent, compassionate, and kind. We can also be, as the Harlem Renaissance poet Langston Hughes put it, "stinkin', low-down, mean."[7]

We have constructive and destructive tendencies. Sometimes we classify each other the way I classified butterflies in the fourth grade.

We invite and disinvite, include and exclude, listen and ignore, heal and abuse, sanctify and scar. We love and hate our diversity.

> **Key questions:** Are you excluding, manipulating, or treating anyone poorly? Is there any area of your life where you are being "stinkin', low-down, mean"?

I've never met an infallible human. Nor have I met a perfect parent, teacher, or coach. Each is a work in progress, an apprentice to greatness. We're all broken, damaged, wounded, and guilty, and yet possess amazing gifts.

It's an idealized notion to think we can undock from society and live deliberately in isolation. The monastic, cloistered alternative never works, and virtual reality is a bubble of indulgence. The truth is, we're embedded in, implicated with, bound to, and shaped by one another. Hannah Arendt wisely observed, "The world lies between people, and this in-between . . . is today the object of the greatest concern and the most obvious upheaval in almost all the countries of the globe."[8]

Crack Yourself Open

Please don't read this book for information. Read it for action. Read it for change. Crack yourself open and look inside. This is a time to summon the courage to conduct a searching, fearless personal inventory. And if you happen to lead a family, team, or organization, conduct an institutional examination of conscience while you're at it.

I have four questions to ask you:

- First, do you truly believe that all men and women are created equal, and do you accept others and welcome them into your society simply because they possess flesh and blood even if their values differ from your own?

- Second, without bias or discrimination, do you encourage others to learn and grow, and do you support them in that process even when they lack confidence or make mistakes?
- Third, do you grant others maximum autonomy to contribute in their own way as they demonstrate their ability to deliver results?
- Fourth, do you consistently invite others to challenge the status quo in order to make things better, and are you personally prepared to be wrong based on the humility and learning mindset you have developed?

These four questions align with the four stages of psychological safety. In large measure, the way you answer these questions will define the way you value human beings and your relationships with them. It will define the way you draw people out or shut them down, create confidence or induce fear, encourage or discourage. It will determine how you lead and influence others.

The philosopher Thomas Hobbes said that there is "a general inclination of all mankind, a perpetual and restless desire of power after power, that ceaseth only in death."[9] That lust for power, wealth, and aggrandizement runs counter to human flourishing because we're connected, not self-contained. "We are," as the former archbishop of Canterbury Rowan Williams said, "healed by relation, not isolation."[10]

Drawing lines of exclusion is not rooted in our biology. It's the adoration of power and distinction, insecurity, and ordinary selfishness that lead us to partition ourselves. As humans, we look for loyalties to attach to. Out of our attachments emerge our differences. Out of our differences emerge our divisions. Out of our divisions emerge our classes, ranks, and stations. And it is out of those spaces between us that the comparisons begin, the empathy flees, the fear and envy emerge, the conflicts arise, the antagonisms gestate, the destructive instincts and impulses for abuse and cruelty arise. In the spirit of our bigotry, we invent dogmas to justify the ways we torment each other.

Ironically, in our digital age, we connect and feel alone, compare and feel inadequate.[11] Indeed, if you have a sudden urge to feel "less than," spend an hour on your favorite social media platform.

> **Key concept:** When you compare and compete, you lose the ability to connect.
>
> **Key question:** Are there any areas in your life where you are losing the ability to connect by making unhelpful or destructive comparisons with others?

Though we can be foul friends to each other, we can also be cool rain on scorched earth—ministers, healers, and good neighbors. We are capable of breathtaking compassion, generosity, and selfless service. I'm not advocating heroism and grand expressions of self-sacrifice. No, my charge to you is, in the most basic sense, to treat human beings as they deserve to be treated—without arbitrary distinctions. Accept them, encourage them, respect them, and allow them. If you want to be happy, come to terms with your fellow creatures. Lose the mock superiority. Stop nursing wrongs and start reaching out. Too many of us live far beneath our privileges, locked in what W. B. Yeats called the "foul rag and bone shop of the heart."[12] If you can create a little more psychological safety for your fellow travelers, it will change your life and theirs. I'm inviting you to change. Change the way you view and treat humanity. The journey I take you on will create both joy and pain. We're never quite ready for that, so the real question is: Are you willing?

The real frontier of modernity is not artificial intelligence; it's emotional and social intelligence. Let me show you why.

Key Concepts

- The leader's task is to simultaneously increase intellectual friction and decrease social friction.

- The presence of fear in an organization is the first sign of weak leadership.
- Psychological safety is a condition in which you feel (1) included, (2) safe to learn, (3) safe to contribute, and (4) safe to challenge the status quo—all without fear of being embarrassed, marginalized, or punished in some way.
- When you compare and compete, you lose the ability to connect.

Key Questions

- Have you ever been dropped into a completely foreign environment? Were you suspicious of the natives? What bias or prejudice did you bring?
- Have you ever been in a position of power? Have you ever been in a position of no power? Did having power or not having power change your behavior?
- Have you ever been a part of an organization that was dominated by fear? How did you respond? How did other people respond?
- Have you ever had the realization that family life is almost always the most challenging place to model and apply correct principles of leadership?
- Do you feel included and listened to at work? How about school? How about home?
- Are you excluding, manipulating, or treating anyone poorly? Is there any area of your life where you are being "stinkin', low-down, mean"? Are there any areas in your life where you are losing the ability to connect by making unhelpful or destructive comparisons with others?
- I'm asking you to change. Change the way you view and treat humanity. The journey I take you on will create both joy and pain. We're never quite ready for that, so the real question is: Are you willing?

The Four Questions

- First, do you truly believe that all men and women are created equal, and do you accept others and welcome them into your society simply because they possess flesh and blood even if their values differ from your own?
- Second, without bias or discrimination, do you encourage others to learn and grow, and do you support them in that process even when they lack confidence or make mistakes?
- Third, do you grant others maximum autonomy to contribute in their own way as they demonstrate their ability to deliver results?
- Fourth, do you consistently invite others to challenge the status quo in order to make things better, and are you personally prepared to be wrong based on the humility and learning mindset you have developed?

Introduction

I spent my early boyhood in Durango, Colorado. My father was a teacher among the Navajo, the second-largest Native American tribe next to the Cherokee. Although we were not Native Americans, not members of the tribe, and not speakers of Navajo, these people welcomed us into their society. The cultural differences between us were significant, and they didn't magically disappear, yet they accepted us—not suddenly, but gradually—by extending bonds of affection and a sense of belonging that I clearly perceived as a child. They included us, and we could feel that sense of inclusion.

On one occasion I went with my father to a remote part of the reservation. As we drove by a small settlement, we saw a man standing outside. Dad stopped the truck and walked over to greet the man, knowing that if he didn't stop, it might create suspicion because it was unusual for non–Native Americans to wander through this isolated place. I stayed in the truck and observed the exchange. The men didn't shake hands. No salutations of any kind. Nor could I see on the face of the Navajo man any nonverbal cues to indicate his mood or response. He seemed emotionless, and that flat affect led me to believe that he was not happy. Without a smile or wave, the men simply parted. By the time my father returned to the truck, I was sure he had offended the man.

> **Key question:** Have you ever misjudged another person because you didn't understand cultural differences?

"Is he mad?" I asked, as my father got back in the truck.

My father gave me a puzzled look and responded, "He said we could stay on his land and bathe in his stream."

I had misinterpreted the entire exchange.

Before we come in contact with each other, we're in a state of separation but not a state of exclusion. We are strangers but not estranged. Whenever human beings begin interacting, they begin the process of deciding if and how they will accept each other into their respective societies. The way we accept or reject, include or exclude, takes many forms, but the primary way we draw lines among us is by granting or withholding psychological safety. Let me repeat the definition:

> **Key concept:** Psychological safety is a condition in which you feel (1) included, (2) safe to learn, (3) safe to contribute, and (4) safe to challenge the status quo—all without fear of being embarrassed, marginalized, or punished in some way.

The concept of psychological safety is as old as the first human interaction. But it's only been in recent years that we have consolidated the concept under a unifying term since the psychologist William Kahn first coined it in 1990. Other pioneering researchers such as Edgar Schein, Warren Bennis, and Amy Edmondson have helped us understand how and why psychological safety is directly related to team performance and business impact.[1] In the past we used other terms to identify psychological safety and its antecedents. For example, Carl Rogers spoke of the need for "unconditional positive regard."[2] Douglas McGregor referred to nonphysical "security needs."[3] The Nobel Prize laureate Herbert Simon suggested that fully functioning organizations require "attitudes of friendliness and cooperation."[4] And finally, if you go back to Abraham Maslow, he identified "belongingness needs," stating that, "if both the physiological and the safety needs are fairly well gratified, then there will emerge the love and affection and belongingness needs."[5]

Psychological safety is a postmaterialist need, but it is no less a human need than food or shelter. In fact, you could argue that psycholog-

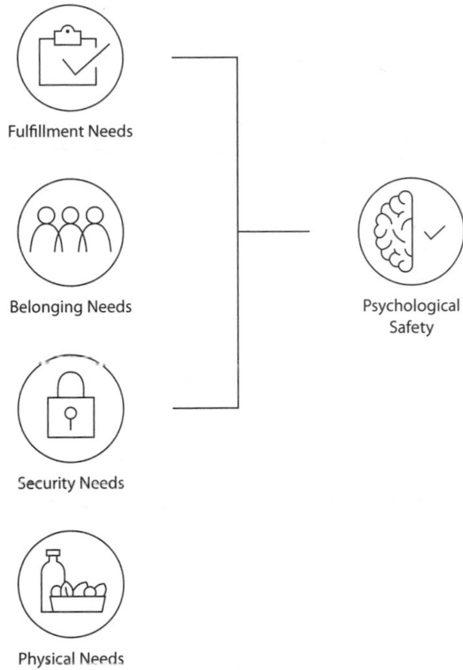

Figure 3: Psychological safety and the hierarchy of needs

ical safety is simply the manifestation of the need for self-preservation in a social and emotional sense. Or you might call it industrialized love. Eric Fromm explained, "Unless he [referring to both women and men] belonged somewhere, unless his life had some meaning and direction, he would feel like a particle of dust and be overcome by his individual insignificance. He would not be able to relate himself to any system which would give meaning and direction to his life, he would be filled with doubt, and this doubt eventually would paralyze his ability to act—that is, to live."[6]

In the hierarchy of needs, psychological safety straddles fulfillment, belonging, and security needs—three of the four basic need categories (figure 3). Once the basic physical needs of food and shelter are met, psychological safety becomes a priority.

Key question: Are there areas of your life where a lack of psychological safety limits your ability to act, live, and be happy?

Think of a time when you were embarrassed, marginalized, or otherwise rejected in a social setting—a teacher ignored your question, a boss criticized your idea, a coworker mocked your English pronunciation, a casting director ridiculed your audition, a coach yelled at you for making an unforced error, your team ditched you and went to lunch. I'm referring to times when you were deprived of psychological safety. Do you remember those wounding experiences? They're sticky because they sting.

Do those occasions influence your behavior? As the sociologist Arlie Russell Hochschild reminds us, "Feeling is a form of pre-action."[7] When we're snubbed, ignored, silenced, brushed off, ostracized, or humiliated; when we're bullied, harassed, or shamed; when we're scorned, passed over, or neglected, those experiences are not neutral events. They're demoralizing, lead to alienation, and activate the pain centers of the brain. They crush confidence and leave us in resentful, stupefied silence. In fact, sometimes the fear of these things can be more debilitating than the actual thing. Clearly, how we feel influences what we think and do.

Not given a voice and being mistreated can have a profound impact on our ability to perform, create value, and thrive. As humans, we instinctively sense the vibe, tone, and atmosphere around us and respond accordingly. But it's not a binary proposition—psychological safety is not something you either have or don't. From the nuclear family to the Navy SEALs, from the food truck to the president's cabinet—every social unit registers some level of psychological safety.

In organizations, it's an uncontested finding that high psychological safety drives performance and innovation, while low psychological safety incurs the disabling costs of low productivity and high attrition. Google's Project Aristotle proved that IQ points and money don't necessarily produce results. After studying 180 of its teams, Google found that smarts and resources can't compensate for what a team may lack in psychological safety. In fact, the company landed on psychological safety as the single most important factor in explaining high performance.[8]

Key concept: An organization that expects employees to bring their whole selves to work should engage the whole employee.

When psychological safety is high, people take more ownership and release more discretionary effort, resulting in higher-velocity learning and problem solving. When it's low, people don't muscle through the fear. Instead, they shut down, self-censor, and redirect their energy toward risk management, pain avoidance, and self-preservation. As Celia Swanson, a former executive vice president at Walmart, said, "Making the decision to speak up against a toxic culture is one of the most difficult decisions employees may face in their careers."[9]

Key concept: In the twenty-first century, high psychological safety will increasingly become a term of employment, and organizations that don't supply it will bleed out their top talent.

My fieldwork with organizations across industries, cultures, and demographics has led me to identify a consistent pattern in the ways that social units grant psychological safety and how individuals perceive it. There's a natural progression across four developmental stages based on a combination of respect and permission. By *respect*, I mean the general level of regard and esteem we give each other. To respect someone is to value and appreciate them. By *permission*, I mean the permission given to others to participate as members of a social unit, the degree to which we allow them to influence us and participate in what we are doing.

As organizations grant increasing levels of respect and permission, individuals generally behave in a way that reflects the level of psychological safety offered to them. Each stage encourages individuals to

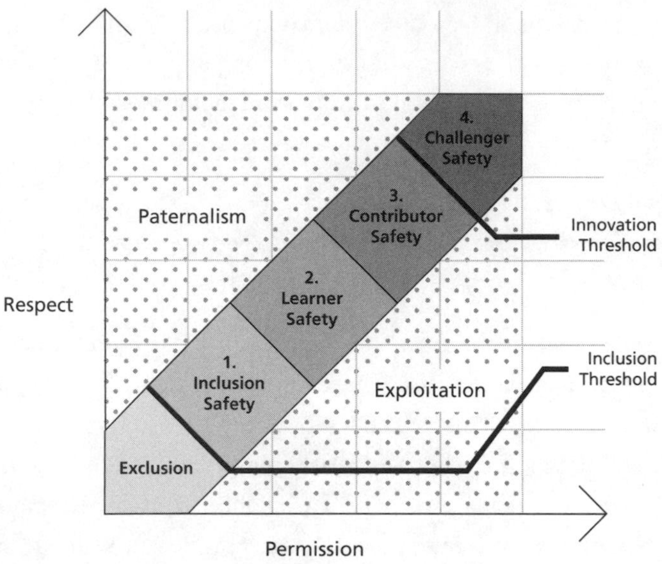

Figure 4. The path from inclusion to innovation

engage more and accelerate both their personal development and the value-creation process.

> **Key concept:** People flourish when they're participating in a cooperative system with high psychological safety.

The "four stages of psychological safety" framework can be used as a diagnostic tool to assess the stage of psychological safety in any organization or social unit (figure 4). The following explanations of each stage are only summaries. I'll spend the remainder of the book exploring each of the four stages in greater detail.

Stage 1 Inclusion Safety

The first stage of psychological safety is informal admittance to the team—whether it's the neighborhood book club or the College of Cardinals. In other words, the members of the social collective accept you and grant you a shared identity. You are now destigmatized as an outsider and brought into the fold. But it's important to understand that inclusion safety isn't merely tolerance; it's not an attempt to cover up differences or politely pretend they're not there. No, inclusion safety is provided by genuinely inviting others into your society based on the sole qualification that they possess flesh and blood. This transcendent connection supersedes all other differences.

Key concept: The need to be accepted precedes the need to be heard.

As a species, we have both natural instincts and acquired socialization to detect social boundaries as well as gestures of invitation or rejection across those boundaries—to perceive the levels of respect and permission offered to us.

For example, when a new high school student asks her peers, "Can I eat lunch with you guys?" The response to that question extends inclusion safety if the students say yes. If they say no, the individual is not allowed to cross the threshold of inclusion. In a more subtle version of this encounter, the student is simply ignored by her peers as she passes by. In some cases, we ignore each other as a gentle way to pour scorn. Regardless, it hurts when you're cast off and acceptance is denied. As one poignant example of the acute need for inclusion, an American College Health Association survey of undergraduate college students found that 63 percent of the students surveyed reported feeling "very lonely." That's nearly two-thirds of the student population.[10] In spite of our material plenty, we increasingly suffer from social and emotional poverty.[11]

Key concept: Being ignored is often as painful as being rejected.

William James, the father of American psychology said, "No more fiendish punishment could be devised, were such a thing physically possible, than that one should be turned loose in society and remain absolutely unnoticed by all the members thereof. If not one turned around when we entered, answered when we spoke, or minded what we did, but if every person we met 'cut us dead,' and acted as if we were nonexistent things, a kind of rage and impotent despair would before long well up in us, from which the cruelest bodily torture would be a relief."[12]

Why do active shooters kill innocent victims? Why do citizens spew vitriol and hate? Why has the suicide rate in the United States increased by 33 percent in just the last eighteen years?[13] Directly linked to alienation, disaffection, and ostracism, these tragic outcomes result from deeply unmet needs. Clearly, granting and receiving inclusion safety is a matter not only of happiness but, indeed, life and death.

> **Key concept:** When human beings can't gain acceptance or approval from each other, they often seek attention as a replacement, even if that attention is destructive.

Inclusion safety is created and sustained through renewed admittance to the group and repeated indications of acceptance. In the business world, we are formally admitted to a team when we're hired, but informal membership is granted or withheld by the people with whom we work. You may be the new hire on the software development team, which gives you official membership status, but you still need the team's sociocultural acceptance to gain inclusion safety. Giving inclusion safety is a moral imperative.

Stage 2 Learner Safety

Learner safety indicates that you feel safe to engage in the discovery process, ask questions, experiment, and even make mistakes—not if, but when, you make them. Without learner safety, you will likely remain passive due to the risk of acting beyond a tacit line of permission. In children, adolescents, and adults, the patterns are the same: We all bring inhibitions and anxiety to the learning process.

> **Key concept:** When the environment belittles, demeans, or harshly corrects people in the learning process, learner safety is destroyed.

An environment that grants safe passage to learning opens the buds of potential, cultivating confidence, resilience, and independence.

While individuals can remain relatively passive in the stage of inclusion safety, learner safety requires them to exert themselves and develop self-efficacy. They are no longer spectators. The transition to learner safety means crossing into the anxiety of the unknown. When learner safety is present, the leader and team may even supply some of the confidence that the individual lacks. For instance, days after the French philosopher Albert Camus won the Nobel Prize in literature in 1957, he wrote a letter of gratitude to his elementary school teacher. He said, "Dear Monsieur Germain, Without you, without the affectionate hand you extended to the small poor child that I was, without your teaching and example, none of this would have happened."[14]

Learner safety implies activity and participation within defined limits. For example, I observed an apprentice plumber assisting a more experienced master plumber at a job site. The apprentice was given learner safety to observe, ask questions, prepare tools and materials, and contribute in a limited way to the work. As the master plumber responded positively to the apprentice's questions, the apprentice released more discretionary effort to learn, do, and become.

In a contrasting case, I watched a hotel manager's frustration escalate with a front desk clerk who was trying to resolve a pressing customer problem. The more questions the clerk asked, the more frustrated the manager became. That frustration replaced respect and permission, creating an emotional barrier that shut down the clerk's willingness to ask more questions and initiate action. As expected, the clerk began to behave as a compliant victim, losing both initiative and enthusiasm.

Stage 3 Contributor Safety

As individual performances climb higher in a nurturing environment that offers respect and permission, we enter the stage of contributor safety, which invites the individual to participate as an active and full-fledged member of the team. Contributor safety is an invitation and an expectation to perform work in an assigned role with appropriate boundaries, on the assumption that you can perform competently in your role. If you don't offend the social norms of the team, you're normally granted contributor safety when you gain competency in the required skills and assigned tasks.

Key concept: As the individual demonstrates competence, the organization normally grants more autonomy to contribute.

The transition to contributor safety may also be tied to credentials, title, position, and the formal conferral of authority. For example, when a coach selects a player on an athletic team to join the starting lineup, there's often an immediate transition to contributor safety. When a hospital hires a well-qualified surgeon, she's formally granted contributor safety. Thus, where formal authority or credentials are prerequisite to a role, they act as partial proxy for psychological safety based on the official or legal right to contribute.

Despite an ability to do the job, an individual may nonetheless be denied contributor safety for illegitimate reasons, including the arrogance or insecurity of the leader, personal or institutional bias, prejudice or discrimination, prevailing team norms that reinforce insensitivity, a lack of empathy, or aloofness. Contributor safety emerges when the individual performs well, but the leader and team must do their part to provide encouragement and appropriate autonomy.

Stage 4 Challenger Safety

The final stage of psychological safety allows you to challenge the status quo without retribution, reprisal, or the risk of damaging your personal standing or reputation. It gives you the confidence to speak truth to power when you think something needs to change and it's time to say so. Armed with challenger safety, individuals overcome the pressure to conform and can enlist themselves in the creative process.

Analyzing its massive database of more than fifty thousand skills, LinkedIn conducted a study to identify the most important soft skills. Can you guess what skill was most in demand? Answer: creativity.[15] But creativity is never enough. Only when people feel free and able do they apply their creativity. Each of us protects our creativity under emotional lock and key. We turn the key from the inside out—when it's safe to do so. Without challenger safety, there's little chance of that because threats, judgement, and other limiting beliefs block curiosity in ourselves and others.

> **Key question:** How likely are you to innovate if you don't perceive high levels of respect and permission around you?

A middle manager from a global corporation summed it up this way, "I'm very careful to stick my neck out and challenge the status quo. If I do and don't get my head chopped off, I'll do it again. If I get my head chopped off, you can rest assured I'll keep my ideas to myself."

This statement illustrates the self-censoring instinct all humans possess and the inherent competitive advantage that challenger safety provides. The open climate of challenger safety allows the organization to circulate local knowledge from the bottom of the organization to the top to increase its adaptive capacity. But that's not all: it also empowers people to be curious and creative.

If you conduct a postmortem analysis of failure for almost any commercial organization that dies, you can trace the cause of death to a lack of challenger safety. For example, why did Kodak, Blockbuster,

Palm, Borders, Toys "R" Us, Circuit City, Atari, Compaq, Radio Shack, and AOL fail? They lost their competitive advantage by failing to innovate, but why? These organizations were filled with large numbers of highly intelligent people, and yet they all fell prey to competitive threats that were hiding in plain sight. The countervailing strategies their competitors put in place were not mysterious. They were, in fact, obvious. What these organizations failed to do was challenge the status quo and disrupt themselves. They were, as Thoreau observed, "buried in the grave of custom." They allowed the status quo to fossilize and would not allow themselves to change it.

The process of scrutinizing the status quo normally injects a degree of conflict, confrontation, and sometimes a measure of chaos. When there's censure or punishment, when intellectual conflict turns into interpersonal conflict, when fear becomes a motivator, the process collapses and people go silent.

Key concept: Where there is no tolerance for candor, there is no constructive dissent. Where there is no constructive dissent, there is no innovation.

Challenger safety is a license to innovate. It's the leader's job to manage the tension and draw out the collective genius of people, and then sustain that recursive process through trial and error. Brilliance emerges from the interdependence of the team. But organizations are often reluctant to grant challenger safety because it threatens the power structure, allocation of resources, incentives, reward system, and speed of operation. Innovation is the lifeblood of growth and yet a formidable cultural challenge. Some organizations never get it. Others get it and then lose it. "Organizations have habits," Brad Anderson, the CEO of Best Buy, observes, "and they will cling to their habits at the expense sometimes of their own survival."[16] This pattern is true at an individual level as well.

Key question: What fossilized habits do you have that you need to change?

For many leaders, asking for something that makes them personally vulnerable is beyond their moral, emotional, and intellectual capacity. That's why they're unable to cross the threshold of innovation and create this high level of psychological safety in their organizations. Consider the *Challenger* space shuttle disaster caused by the failure of O-ring seals used in the field joints of the solid rocket boosters. The seals were not designed to function properly under the cold conditions that existed on the day of launch. Experts warned NASA not to launch the shuttle at temperatures below 53 degrees, but feeling the pressure of previous launch delays, senior leadership silenced the detractors, dismissed warnings, and proceeded. Arrogance and a lack of challenger safety contributed to the tragedy.

As I work with leaders in organizations that operate in highly dynamic environments, those that create challenger safety gain a competitive advantage because they are able to accelerate the process of innovation. Those prone to cherish formal status and amass power cannot because they don't, as chess grandmaster Gary Kasparov said, "have the guts to explode the game." Unable to embrace vulnerability, sacrifice personal interests, and escape their ego needs, they're not up to the job.

Finally, to scale innovation throughout the organization, leaders must establish a norm of challenging the status quo. No technology-enabled suggestion box or collaborative jam session will work without underlying challenger safety. And keep in mind that not responding to a suggestion can be worse than outright rejection—which is at least an acknowledgment.

In the twenty-first century, the need for challenger safety is becoming more important as accelerating markets squeeze the average span of competitive advantage. In 1966, the average tenure of an S&P 500 company was thirty-three years. It shrank to twenty-four years by 2016 and is projected to plummet to twelve years by the year 2027.[17]

The assumption going forward is that this trend will continue without a new equilibrium or state of normalcy. Except for a few organizations that seem to have an impenetrable moat of competitive advantage, organizations will need to create and sustain challenger safety as the incubating force that enables perpetual innovation. Without it, they won't have the agility to compete.

What if an organization has not purged its legacy of prejudice toward women, minorities, religious identities, or other human characteristics? Most organizations grant equality and inclusion as a matter of policy; few live and breathe it as a matter of culture and behavior. How, then, can an organization convert diversity in composition into active, confident, and vibrant diversity in action? Without psychological safety, intellectual diversity will lie fallow. Those who live and work in the shadows will repress their instinct to explore. They won't engage in constructive dissent because they've never seen it done. Nor have they been granted the respect and permission to participate.

The Bowling Lane and the Gutters

What happens when a team grants some respect or permission to its members, but not both—when the pattern of psychological safety moves out of the bowling lane, so to speak, into the gutter on one side or the other? (Refer back to Figure 4 to note the location of paternalism and exploitation in the framework.)

When a team offers a measure of respect, but very little permission, it falls into the gutter of paternalism. Paternalistic leaders act like helicopter parents and benevolent dictators who micromanage their children, patting them on the head and telling them not to touch things. Early in my career, the CEO of a small company for which I worked asked the members of our team for feedback concerning the organization. I misread the signals and mistakenly believed I had been granted challenger safety, spending several hours preparing a memo. I never heard back from the CEO and later learned from my colleagues that such a request was not genuine. I also learned from my own feelings that paternalism breeds cynicism and disengagement.

Key question: Do you see evidence of paternalism in your family, school, or workplace in which people micromanage others and leave them powerless?

On the other hand, what happens when a team grants a measure of permission to contribute, but little respect? In this case, the team falls into the gutter of exploitation—a condition in which the leader attempts to extract value while not valuing those who create the value. Taken to an extreme, this is slavery and the sweatshop. But there are everyday examples all around us in the form of shaming, harassing, and bullying behavior. You would think it would incite a populist revolt, and yet people routinely endure this mistreatment out of fear of losing their jobs.

Key questions: Do you see evidence of people taking advantage of others in your family, school, or workplace? Has shaming, harassing, or bullying behavior become normalized?

As a plant manager, I often witnessed a command-and-control, fear-and-intimidation style of leadership that had little regard for humanity and regarded workers as commoditized flesh. As a result, I found myself classifying managers as either net consumers or net contributors. Consumers consume. It's their chief impulse. They tend to view everything and everyone as means to their own gratification and regard leadership as a pathway to their own indulgence. Their leadership paradigm is built on the premise that they're better or more deserving than the other members of the species.

In the other camp, we find contributors. They arrive ready to serve, build, encourage, and make things better. They, too, are driven to achieve personal success, but here's the difference: They stop short of using or sacrificing others to do it. Refusing to step on another person's neck to get what they want, they carry a burning conviction that human beings are the ends, never a means.

Conclusion

I see uncritical celebrations of diversity everywhere, but diversity produces nothing and blesses no one unless its value can be drawn out. A leader's most important job—above that of creating a vision and setting strategy—is to act in the role of social architect and nourish a context in which people are given the respect and permission to (1) feel included, (2) learn, (3) contribute, and (4) innovate. It's the culminating stage of both leadership development and organizational culture to create and sustain this kind of environment.

Key concept: Organizations don't outperform their leaders, they reflect them.

Creating psychological safety depends on setting the tone and modeling the behavior. You either show the way or get in the way. If you can learn to harvest the full fruit of psychological safety, you will transform families, schools, organizations, and societies, enabling people to realize their deep yearnings—to live happy, connected, creative, contributing, and more beautiful lives.

Key Concepts

- Psychological safety is a condition in which you feel (1) included, (2) safe to learn, (3) safe to contribute, and (4) safe to challenge the status quo, all without fear of being embarrassed, marginalized, or punished in some way.
- An organization that expects employees to bring their whole selves to work should engage the whole employee.
- In the twenty-first century, high psychological safety will increasingly become a term of employment, and organizations that don't supply it will bleed out their top talent.

- People flourish when they're participating in a cooperative system with high psychological safety.
- The need to be accepted precedes the need to be heard.
- Being ignored is often as painful as being rejected.
- When human beings can't gain acceptance or approval from each other, they often seek attention as a replacement, even if that attention is destructive in nature.
- When the environment belittles, demeans, or harshly corrects us in the learning process, it destroys learner safety.
- As the individual demonstrates competent performance, the organization normally grants more autonomy to contribute.
- Where there is no tolerance for candor, there is no constructive dissent. Where there is no constructive dissent, there is no innovation.
- Organizations don't outperform their leaders, they reflect them.

Key Questions

- Have you ever misjudged another person because you didn't understand cultural differences?
- Are there areas in your life where a lack of psychological safety limits your ability to act, live, and be happy?
- How likely are you to innovate if you don't perceive high levels of respect and permission?
- What fossilized habits do you have that you need to change?
- Do you see evidence of paternalism in your family, school, or workplace in which people micromanage others and leave them powerless?
- Has shaming, harassing, or bullying behavior become normalized in your family, school, or workplace?

STAGE 1

Inclusion Safety

Our ability to reach unity in diversity will be the beauty and the test of our civilization.

—Mahatma Gandhi

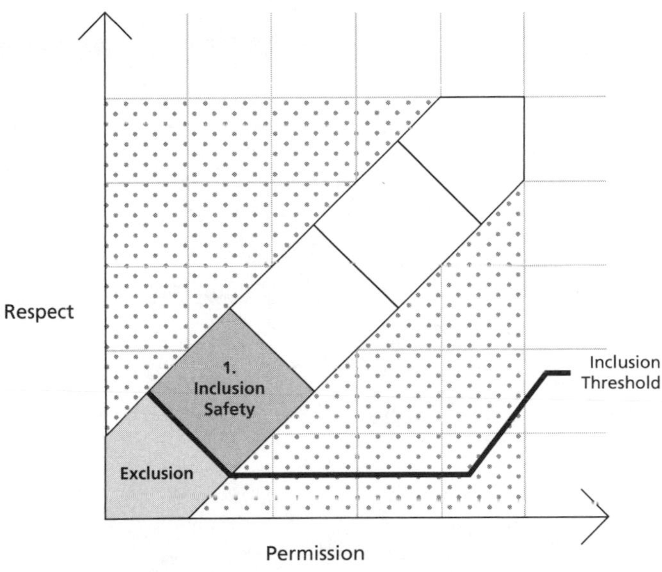

Figure 5. Entering the path to inclusion and innovation

Diversity is a fact. Inclusion is a choice.
But not just any choice.

Key concept: The choice to include another human being activates our humanity.

As the first stage of psychological safety, inclusion safety is, in its purest sense, nothing more than species-based acceptance (figure 5, previous page). If you have flesh and blood, we accept you. Profoundly simple in concept, devilishly difficult in practice, we learn it in kindergarten and unlearn it later. A mere 36 percent of business professionals today believe their companies foster an inclusive culture.[1]

I remember talking to my son, Ben, after his first day of kindergarten:

"How did you like your first day of kindergarten, Ben?" I asked.

"It was fun, Dad."

"Are you excited to go to school tomorrow?"

"Yeah, I'm excited."

"Is Mom going to take you to school again tomorrow?"

"No, I'm going to walk."

"Do you have anyone to walk with?"

"No, Dad, I'll just walk by myself, but if anyone wants to walk with me, they can."

I'll never forget that tender exchange. It's a reflection of the uncorrupted, inclusive nature of children.

Key concept: We include naturally in childhood and exclude unnaturally in adulthood.

Out of our flaws and insecurities, we model and reinforce exclusion to those around us. But it doesn't have to be that way. After living with the Navajo for a few years, my family moved to Los Angeles and then finally settled into a middle-class neighborhood in the San Francisco Bay Area. I remember feeling uprooted and lost as a boy. Bored, lonely, and battling a little resentment, I sat on the porch one day when a kid from the neighborhood rode up on his bike. He walked over and, without any hesitation, announced, "Hi, I'm Kenny." In no time, we were riding our bikes together, eating kumquats, and catching alligator lizards. The young man who befriended me and extended inclusion safety so confidently at age ten is now Pastor Kenny Luck, the men's pastor at the Camelback Church in Lake Forest, California.

Not everyone is born with Kenny's confidence and sense of concern, but the basic decision to include or exclude is not about skill or personality, although those things can enhance your ability to include. It's more about intent than technique. You can't legislate it, regulate it, train it, measure it, or gimmick it into existence. It doesn't answer to those forces. It's an act of will that flows from the empire of the heart. If there's no psychological safety, there's no inclusion.

> **Key concept:** Including another human being should be an act of prejudgment based on that person's worth, not an act of judgment based on that person's worthiness.

Our children memorized passages from Martin Luther King Jr.'s "I Have a Dream" in school. I can still hear them recite the line, "I look to a day when people will not be judged by the color of their skin, but by the content of their character." The theologian Reinhold Niebuhr made a similar observation when he said, "We are admonished in scripture to judge men by their fruits, not by their roots."[2]

Before we judge others as less exalted, please note that the Reverend King and Pastor Niebuhr are talking about worthiness of character.My point is that worth comes first, worthiness comes second. Inclusion safety is not about worthiness. It's about treating people like people. It's the act of extending fellowship, membership, association, and connection—agnostic of rank, status, gender, race, appearance, intelligence, education, beliefs, values, politics, habits, traditions, language, customs, history, or any other defining characteristic. Inclusion marks passage into civilization. If we can't do that as a starting point, we're not being true to what Lincoln called "the better angels of our nature." Withholding inclusion safety is a sign that we're engaged in a fight with our own willful blindness. We're self-medicating with enchanting tales about our distinctiveness and superiority. If it's a mild case of snobbery, that may be easy to dismiss. But if it's a more severe case of narcissistic supremacy, that's a bigger problem. And then there's everything in between.

In our social units, we should create an environment of inclusion before we begin to think about judgments at all. Worth precedes worthiness. There's a time and a place to judge worthiness, but when you allow someone to cross the threshold of inclusion, there's no litmus test. We're not weighing your character in the balance to see if you're found wanting. To be deserving of inclusion has nothing to do with your personality, virtues, or abilities; nothing to do with your gender, race, ethnicity, education or any other demographic variable that defines you. There are, at this level, no disqualifications, except one—the threat of harm.

The only reciprocation requirement in this unwritten social contract is the mutual exchange of respect and permission to belong. That exchange is unenforceable by law. There are, of course, laws against discrimination, but in a thousand ways we can still informally persecute each other.

Let me give you an example of A/B testing for inclusion safety. I have two cars. One is old and rusty, has 315,000 miles on the odometer, and a resale value of $375. The other is a black sports sedan. When I take in my sedan for service, the attendant is highly responsive. When I take my rust bucket, the attendant can be mildly disdainful. In both cases, the car is the lead indicator of my social status, and people grant or withhold inclusion safety based on my car, the artifact in which I sit. Some days I'm politely ignored, some days solicitously attended to. That's how sensitive people are to these indicators because we scramble for status like apes for nuts.

Key questions: Do you treat people that you consider of lower status differently than those of higher status? If so, why?

What should it take to qualify for inclusion safety? Two things: Be human and be harmless. If you meet both criteria, you qualify. If you meet only one, you don't. The great African American abolitionist Frederick Douglass made the definitive statement about inclusion safety when he said, "I know of no rights of race superior to the rights of humanity." That statement can apply to any characteristic. When we extend inclusion safety to each other, we subordinate our differences to invoke a more important binding characteristic—our common humanity.

Table 1 defines respect and permission in the first stage of psychological safety. The definition of *respect* in this stage is simply respect for the individual's humanity. *Permission* in this stage is the permission you give another to enter your personal society and interact with you as a human being. Finally, the social exchange is one in which we trade inclusion for human status, provided we don't threaten each other with harm.

Table 1 **Stage 1 Inclusion Safety**

Stage	Definition of Respect	Definition of Permission	Social Exchange
1. Inclusion Safety	Respect for the individual's humanity	Permission for the individual to enter your personal society	Inclusion in exchange for human status and the absence of harm

Despite knowing we should extend inclusion safety to everyone, we have become very skilled at chasing each other to the margins and patrolling the boundaries. We splinter, segment, and stratify the human family. Sometimes, we extend partial or conditional inclusion safety. Sometimes we revoke or withhold it.

Key concept: Instead of granting inclusion safety based on human status, we tend to judge another person's worthiness based on indicators like appearance, social status, or material possessions, when those indicators have nothing to do with worth.

Kimchi and Our Common Humanity

When I was in graduate school, I had the opportunity to do research at the Seoul National University in Korea as a Fulbright scholar. The university offered me a place at its Social Science Research Center. The day I arrived, Professor Ahn Chung Si greeted me warmly and took me around the center to meet the staff and other researchers. My initial apprehension was replaced with a sense of inclusion when two Korean graduate students asked me to go to lunch. I was the different one, the stranger, the alien, the one that didn't fit in. But I was not the odd person out. Holding my bowl of rice dumpling soup, I sat down at one of the tables in the cafeteria and was soon greeting other students and faculty. With some hesitation, a student sitting next to me handed me a bowl of kimchi. That was the beginning of an extraordinary experience with inclusion safety.

True, I was a novelty, but I hasten to say that inclusion safety is not simply the expression of hospitality. You can be polite and not mean it. That kind of surface acting is a disingenuous way of abiding by common rules of decency and decorum. But these students were not only kind and helpful on my first day, which is easy to do. They were also kind and helpful on my thirtieth day and my sixtieth day and so on. I was clearly outside their social group and overstayed the normal expiration date for standard-protocol, obligatory, respectful treatment. But after weeks and weeks of long days at the center, they never revoked the inclusion safety they first extended. It was real.

Key questions: In the arc of every life are times when inclusion safety makes all the difference, when someone reaches out to include you at a vulnerable time. When did this happen to you? What impact did it have on your life? Are you paying it forward?

Let's put this in historical context. South Korea is considered the world's most neo-Confucian society, historically embracing status hierarchy, inequality, and inherent discrimination as values. Human rights have a short history, but have in recent years been acknowledged as a matter of political expediency, not through some religious or philosophical sense of natural law, inalienability, or God-invested entitlement. In this society, rights are more instrumental than moral, more negotiated than inviolate, more legislated than guaranteed or absolute. Confucianism lacks rational, legal, or moral grounds for inclusion, but rather emphasizes loyalty, devotion, allegiance, and compliance to authority in the promotion of group harmony and stability.

What does all of that mean? It means I'm an outsider. There's no natural place for me in Korean society or hierarchy. And yet my Korean friends included me in a way that superseded their neo-Confucian tradition. They suspended the normal terms of engagement, giving precedence to a higher principle of humanity. Rather than focus on differences, they emphasized common fellowship.[3] Was I now Korean? Did they grant me full social and cultural membership? No. They extended inclusion safety, but on what basis? Was it religious, ethnic, socioeconomic, geographic, cultural, political, legal? None of the above. It was based on a supernal, primordial human connection that overcame our separatism and penetrated to membership in a universal family.

Key question: To create inclusion safety, it helps to understand cultural differences, but you don't need to be an expert in those differences, just sensitive to and appreciative of them. How do you acknowledge and show sensitivity and appreciation for the cultural differences that exist on your team?

Hardening the Concept of Equality

The philosopher John Rawls reminds us of this fundamental truth: "Institutions are just when no arbitrary distinctions are made between persons in the assigning of basic rights and duties."[5] To exclude a member of a social unit based on conscious or unconscious bias is exactly that, an arbitrary distinction. These must be removed, as Rawls says, to "build an enduring system of mutual cooperation."[6]

There will always be differences, but there mustn't be barriers. There will always be majorities and minorities, but we should never attempt to deracinate each other until we melt into a homogenous lot. Our differences define us.

Some would object on grounds that we don't know each other. So how can we accept, include, tolerate, and connect with strangers? And in fact, research shows that the key drivers of psychological safety include familiarity among team members and the quality of those relationships based on prior interactions.[7] To extend inclusion safety is not to extend mature, developed feelings of affection. Your feelings can only be expectant and assumptive, but they can still be real. Xenophobic arguments are born of ignorance, fear, jealousy, or a dishonest desire for superiority.

> **Key concept:** God may have made us of different clay, but there are no grounds to say that your clay is better than mine.

Inclusion safety is not earned but owed. Every human has title to it as a nonnegotiable right. In fact, we can't sustain civilization without it.[8] We hunger for and deserve dignity and esteem from each other and unavoidably practice morality when we extend or withhold inclusion safety. If there's no threat of harm, we should give it without a value judgment. As the basic glue of human society, inclusion safety offers the comforting assurance that you matter. If you're a leader and want your people to perform, you must internalize the universal truth that people want, need, and deserve validation. Inclusion safety requires that we condemn negative bias, arbitrary distinction, or destructive prejudice that refuses to acknowledge our equal worth and the obligation of equal treatment.

If everyone deserves inclusion, if we're all entitled to fellowship and connection, if we have the right to civil and respectful interactions, if the reciprocation of courtesy defines us as a species—we have an obligation to demolish nativism and ethnocentrism. Nations, communities, and organizations aren't the only offenders.[9] We see alienation within families, as individuals shun, banish, and relegate each other to subordinate status. We see parents and children who neglect or harm each other. And then there are the glorious triumphs when we get it right, when we extend the hand of fellowship and are blessed in that moment with the fulfillment of real human connection.

Granting, Withholding, and Revoking Inclusion Safety

After graduating from high school, I took an athletic scholarship to play Division I football at Brigham Young University. Arriving on campus a month early to begin summer training camp, all freshmen players were assigned to live in the same dormitory near the practice facilities. Here was a group of ethnically and culturally diverse young men thrust into a highly structured environment, a para-military boot camp, characterized by sudden and complete immersion.

We surrendered our personal freedom and space, and from that moment would eat, sleep, shower, and sweat together. The machinery of the football regimen dictated every aspect of our daily lives. My teammates represented three primary racial groups—black, white, and Polynesian. But this was nothing new. Despite our coming together from all parts of the country, our racial composition was familiar to most of us. We had been deeply socialized in the ethnically diverse subculture of American football and understood its norms and meritocracy.

The task was to form a new society, one that would organize itself on both Darwinian and communitarian principles. A football team competes with other teams, but its players compete with each other. While the external rivalry was institutional, the internal rivalry was personal. You might be competing with the guy sleeping in the bed next to you. We played a zero-sum, finite game. Introducing the element of competition changes the dynamics of a society and the terms of engagement for granting or withholding inclusion safety. The prevailing norms were at the same time collegial and adversarial, and that duality was maintained throughout the experience. Your teammate could be friend and foe.

The nature of the team-sport environment accelerates the development of familiarity, which is massively important in the formation of psychological safety. As sociometric research from the MIT Human Dynamics Lab attests, the faster and deeper you get to know each other, the more effectively you can work together.[10] More contact and context tend to create more empathy.

On the first day, we bonded slowly, knowing that we would begin practicing and competing the following day. That reality made the collegial and adversarial forces collide. As a result, our initial greetings were warm with fellow players who didn't play our same positions, and chilled with those who did. Every player arrived dripping with honors and recognition, so bluster and bravado were signs of insecurity and a clear signal that a player wasn't as good as advertised.

In what is akin to a modern-day blood sport, you can't carry on a rhetorical career for very long. Performance does the talking. Football was our common aspiration, but the internal competition was a divisive element. We were formally admitted members of the team but extending inclusion safety to each other was an individual matter. Ironically, we admitted or refused to admit each other in the act of joining the society ourselves.

Instead of fusing into a cohesive group, we balkanized into smaller groups based on race or geography. And then of course there were the offensive linemen, who bonded into a unique fraternity of sensitive, industrial-size humans and shut the gates behind them. I, on the other hand, played defensive tackle, where that sort of bonding would violate our gladiator subculture. After a week of what MIT's Edgar Schein would call "spontaneous interaction," you could see norms starting to form.[11] But a week later, the upperclassmen arrived, and our organic society was swallowed up by the larger machine.

When you join an existing organization, as I came to the football team, you inherit a cultural legacy based on perpetuated norms. Unless you're forming a new social collective, you don't start clean. In our case, we freshmen started clean and erected a temporary society that was then abruptly dismantled. When the rest of the team arrived, it was as if the mothership had landed with its cargo of artifacts, habits, customs, mores, and distribution of power. Here came the unyielding orthodoxy and way of doing things, all modeled and reinforced by the coaching staff. Punctuality rule? Enforced. Dress code rule? Not enforced. Respect rule? Enforced. No profanity rule? Not enforced. And so on. As we moved into the regular season, inclusion safety gradually emerged. The internal rivalries settled, and we came together.

Now came the inclusion safety lesson of a lifetime: Halfway into the season, I sustained a serious injury. When the diagnosis came back that I had severely damaged my ankle and needed surgery, I experienced a sudden and dramatic change in status. My position coach revoked inclusion safety through a silent campaign of neglect. I was injured and therefore unable to contribute to the team. To him I was now invisible. He had extended conditional inclusion safety to me, not based on my worth as a human being, but rather on my worthiness as a player. The moment I got hurt and was no longer useful to the team, he withdrew his fellowship through subtle and unmistakable indifference. That indifference stung. As I quickly learned, inclusion safety, once built, is fragile, delicate, and impermanent.

Key concept: In any social unit, inclusion safety can be granted, withheld, revoked, or partially or conditionally granted.

Soothing Ourselves with Junk Theories of Superiority

Theories have consequences. Too often we have run our societies on intellectually unclean theories. Regardless of the society you live in, the historian's pen has shown that nearly every society has its origins in bigotry, discrimination, conquest, servitude, and exploitation. Governments and rulers have spent much of their time spinning theories of superiority to justify their grip on power. To make it respectable and give it the illusion of morality, they package privilege and power as political ideology.[12] We do the same thing at a personal level as we marinate in notions of supremacy and award ourselves elevated status.

Key concept: We like to tell ourselves soothing stories to justify our sense of superiority.

Theories of superiority are attempts to show how, in the words of George Orwell, "All animals are equal, but some animals are more equal than others." I remember reading Hitler's *Mein Kampf* as a student. I had to hold my nose but I kept reading because I was fascinated that this clever work of eugenics-based grandiosity had influenced so many people. It's beguiling when someone tells you that you're better than everyone else, that you've been unjustly dealt with, and that you deserve more.

It's the same facile thesis we find in all theories of superiority and biological determinism, and all attempts at intellectual imperialism. It begins with a false claim of superiority, or election, on some grounds, and then moves to a call to action: you're in the minority, you're in danger, and you need to rise up and defend yourself. Unfortunately, absurd strains of social Darwinism have always been effective when presented with urgency and erudition. People fall for it. And it really doesn't matter whose theory of superiority you read; they're all meditations in hypocrisy, bathed in jingoism, resting on the same veiled attempts to preserve the vassalage of the past.

Key question: Do you feel superior to other people? If so, why?

Shocking as it may sound, theories of superiority have dominated human societies for millennia. As one of the first power theorists, Aristotle declared, "It is clear that some men are by nature free and others by nature slaves, and that for these latter, slavery is both expedient and right."[13] We have libraries filled with theories of superiority because we have an irrepressible desire to be just a little more special than the next person. John Adams wrote, "I believe there is no one principle which predominates in human nature so much in every stage of life, from the cradle to the grave, in males and females, old and young, black and white, rich and poor, high and low, as this passion for superiority."[14]

With history to ponder, how can we excuse ourselves on the premise that human nature is full of paradoxes, contradictions, and complexities. It's dangerous and incorrect to dismiss the natural-rights tradition as just one of many propaganda traditions. How many times have we dressed up vanity as moral philosophy? How many times have we disguised elitism as the naturally stratified order of heaven?

Thankfully, many people don't subscribe to these pretensions. But many do. In our modern society, we have long since repudiated the grand theories of bloodline aristocracy, but we continue to hatch, nurse, and perpetuate informal versions that do the same thing. They show up as stereotype, resentment, bias, and prejudice and linger in our values, assumptions, and behavior.

When I began my service as plant manager at Geneva Steel, I conducted a series of tours throughout the plant. I traveled from facility to facility, holding town hall meetings, greeting the managers and production and maintenance workers. I started at the coke plant, and then moved to the blast furnaces, steel-making operations, casting, rolling mills, finishing units, shipping and transportation, and central maintenance.

In the coke plant, two production workers cornered me. They removed their hard hats and safety goggles, revealing faces caked with sweat and soot. "Mr. Clark," they said deferentially, "thank you for coming to visit our department. We know you're new to your position as plant manager. We know you're going to visit all the departments, but we just wanted you to know that our department is a little different than the others. Our department is a little more complicated than the others, and it requires a little more expertise to do what we do. If we weren't here, the plant would shut down tomorrow." They made their case and stated their claim. I politely responded, "Thank you for sharing that with me. I appreciate your feedback."

That scene repeated itself in every department. The faces were different, but the script was the same. After my weeklong tour, I was illuminated with the revelation that every department was just a little more important than the others, occupied by a special class of people, doing what no one else could do. They all gently shunted their brothers and sisters in order to distinguish themselves. I suppose we have all made, or been tempted to make, a similar claim and fallen prey to the grand illusion of superiority.

Key questions: Is the moral principle of inclusion a convenient or inconvenient truth for you?

The Elite and the Great Unwashed

The US Constitution lights the world with an unequivocal declaration of human rights, but it's taken generations to find the courage to unwind legalized discrimination and dismantle the edifice of false superiority. In 1776, Abigail Adams wrote her husband, John, "I desire that you would Remember the Ladies. We will not have ourselves bound by any Laws in which we have no voice, or Representation." Two years later, the original American colonies ratified the US Constitution. Although the document was the first government charter that acknowledged the equality of all human beings, it carved out exceptions and violated the ideals it espoused, allowing slavery, counting slaves as equal to a three-fifths of a "normal" human, and not least, withholding voting rights from women. Nor could women own property, keep their own wages, or, in some states, even choose their own husbands. The US Constitution decreed inclusion, but too often we practiced exclusion. It would still take many generations to internalize the espoused values because theories of superiority were deeply ingrained in the American psyche as they were in every nation.[15] Consider the following official acts of exclusion:

- Congress passed the Naturalization Act of 1790, declaring that only white people could become citizens of the nation.
- Congress passed the Indian Removal Act of 1830 to drive out Native Americans from their tribal lands.
- Lincoln issued the Emancipation Proclamation in 1863, but states passed Jim Crow laws to enforce discrimination, and the Supreme Court piled on with its "separate but equal" legal doctrine.
- In 1882, Congress passed the Chinese Exclusion Act, barring Chinese immigration.
- In 1910, 1.6 million children aged ten to fifteen worked in factories. The Fair Labor Standards Act didn't ban child labor until 1938.
- Women did not win the right to vote until we passed the Nineteenth Amendment in 1920.
- In 1942, President Franklin D. Roosevelt authorized the evacuation and incarceration of 127,000 Japanese Americans from the West Coast to internment camps.
- Hispanic American workers didn't gain the right to unionize until the 1950s.
- Ultimately, we didn't purge deliberate and systematic prejudice out of our immigration laws until the Immigration Act of 1965.

But what about our culture? We continue to struggle to redress inequality and forsake notions of male and Anglo-Saxon supremacy.

As my teenage daughter asks, "Dad, why is gender wage equity still a thing?"

We have purged most of our policies of discrimination, but have our hearts changed? Have we become a more inclusive society? A recent EY study reports that less than half of employees trust their bosses and employers.[16] Where there's no trust, there's exclusion. This number is troubling because we know that trust is what binds us together.[17] If familiarity based on frequency of interaction has this amazing ability to eliminate bias and distrust, why are trust numbers so low?

This is the "society versus community" dichotomy.[18] We would expect to see a trusting community within a more distrustful society. There should be proportionately more trust as we move to smaller social units. Organizations should have more trust than governments. Teams should have more than organizations. Families should have more than teams, and marriages should have the most. There should be more good faith and lower transaction costs in our interactions as we move from big to small.[19] If this is true, and I think it is, we get nowhere until we grant each other inclusion safety.

Who's getting in the way? The psychologist Carol Dweck has said, "Your failures and misfortunes don't threaten other people. It's your assets and your successes that are problems for people who derive their self-esteem from being superior."[20] The irony is that because of our insecurity we refuse to validate each other, which is the very thing that heals the insecurity. That unmet need expresses itself in jealousy, resentment, and contempt. Meanwhile, society is filled to overflowing with incivility, and hate has become a growth industry.

> **Key concept:** Excluding a person is more often the result of personal unmet needs and insecurities than a genuine dislike of the person.

How many times have you been suspicious or critical of someone you didn't really know, and when you got to know that person, your entire attitude changed? Differences tend to repel us initially, but when we suspend judgment, we can bridge those differences. When I was in college, I took a class from a professor with radical views and braced myself for combat. I went to class and learned that this gentleman did indeed hold views very different from my own, but we developed a wonderful Ruth Bader Ginsberg–Antonin Scalia–like friendship. We had marvelous disagreements but maintained a deep respect for each other. If we don't watch ourselves, there are a thousand ways to withhold inclusion safety. And if we dehumanize each other, we give ourselves permission to hate and harm each other.

I once worked with an executive team whose members had withdrawn inclusion safety from each other. They were legal officers of a corporation but had revoked each other's cultural passports. The team was dysfunctional. They would verbally bruise and bludgeon each other and could barely stand to be in the same room. In my interview with one of them, she said, "We don't have to like each other; we just have to work together, so I guess it doesn't really matter. I'm all about getting the job done. I don't care too much about the relationships anyway."

I worked with another leader who asserted dominance through an arbitrary pattern of giving and revoking inclusion safety. You were in his good graces one day, out the next, respected then neglected, heard then ignored, fawned over then forgotten, coached then coerced, healed then hurt. Let's be clear: head games are a form of abuse in which one human toys with another. That pattern of interaction is moral cowardice at its finest.

Family as the Realm of Thick Trust

The word *accept* means to consent to receive. The word *inclusion* means having the status of association or connection to a group. Now think about these two words as it relates to the family unit. The relationship between husband and wife is based on the consent to receive the other. The family unit that is created from that union is a new entity to which both are parties. If one spouse denies membership to the other, the social unit doesn't function. The legal tie that binds them together may be intact, but the reality of their union has evaporated.

The interdependence of the marriage relationship is more fundamental than in any other social collective. It is fragile and yet designed to be the realm of the thickest trust. At any moment, one party may withdraw inclusion safety from the other. The respect and permission to participate that each gives the other is the very basis of their interdependency, their success, and their happiness. That inclusion safety is dynamic and perishable. It must be replenished every day. Particularly in marriage, respect must be translated into acts of kindness, service, and sacrifice. Without a consistent investment in gestures of respect, the relationship will wither from neglect. But in a coequal partnership, in which both spouses participate and permit the other equal power and participation rights, the relationship is likely to produce sustainable, high levels of inclusion safety and a deeply fulfilling experience for both.

The relationship between parents and children is somewhat different. Children begin life in a stage of dependence and hopefully move to a stage of interdependence as they learn and grow. A stage of pure independence is of course a fiction. In the development process, the intersection of love and accountability is all important. Parents shouldn't condone poor behavior, but neither should they condemn the child for it. The child is much more able to learn both rights and responsibility in a nurturing environment of sustained inclusion safety. It's over the elusive combination of love and accountability that so many of us stumble. I've stumbled many times, but often to my children's dismay, I've learned to say, "I love you and I'm going to hold you accountable" in the same sentence and mean it.

Key questions: The basic social unit of the family is the primary laboratory for gaining a true civic education in inclusion safety. Did you learn it in your family? If not, do you intend to be a transformational figure in your family and model inclusion safety for the next generation?

Behave until You Believe

What if you can't find the conviction to include someone? What if you have a deep-seated bias or prejudice that you can't dislodge from your heart? How do you overcome it? Where do we find, to use Kafka's phrase, "the ax for the frozen sea within us"?[21] One thing that doesn't work very well is to sit back and wait for your heart to change.

There's not a person alive without at least some trace elements of negative bias against some human characteristic. But some of us are more blameworthy than others. We need to be honest about the acquisition of bias and prejudice and work hard to remove it. We don't get to make choices about diversity; diversity simply is. It's our job to embrace it.

> **Key questions:** What conscious bias do you have? Ask a trusted friend where you may have unconscious bias. Finally, where do you exercise soft forms of exclusion to maintain barriers?

Learn to love yourself first. People with low self-regard have a hard time being inclusive. Whatever your level of self-regard, it spills into your interpersonal behavior. As Nathaniel Branden observes, "Research shows that a well-developed sense of personal value and autonomy correlates significantly with kindness, generosity, social cooperation, and a spirit of mutual aid."[22] The best and quickest way to develop self-regard is to develop your own capacity and confidence and to perform acts of service for others, especially for those whom you struggle to include.

Think about the traditional approaches most organizations take to diversity and inclusion. Many organizations have made great strides to create diverse organizations, but they're still not inclusive. Others achieve a token representation of the full range of human differences and congratulate themselves as if they have an inclusive culture. Still others train employees to be inclusive by teaching them awareness, understanding, and appreciation for differences. That's nice, but it's a coat of paint.[23] When we feel threatened, we get defensive, take counsel from our fears, and go back to our default settings of learned bias. A better way is to give people opportunities to practice inclusion. Make it experiential by creating diverse teams and assigning individuals to diverse mentoring or peer coaching relationships.

Key concept: You learn inclusion when you practice inclusion. Behave until you believe.

Inclusive behavior produces its own confirming evidence.[24] The call to action is simple: affirm the individual worth of other human beings. Do I mean fake it until you feel it? Lease your kindness? Pretend? Wear the mask of an inclusive person? No, I mean earnest striving with real intent.

Key concept: As you love people with action, you come to love them with emotion.

The feeling of love is the reward of the action of love. In fact, if we fail to serve others, our relationships remain superficial, and even suspicious, until we close the distance. In that closeness, in living, working, eating, and breathing together, regard and affection finally arrive. If you don't feel the way you want to feel, or know you should feel, toward an individual or group, the passage of time won't change that, but your actions will. Act yourself into the emotion of love.

I've lived and worked with people from all parts of the world. I love them all and yet I realize that every nation, society, and family thinks it's special. If we take *special* to mean singular or unique, I wholeheartedly agree. But if we take it to mean that we are better than our neighbors, I know where that comes from. We all want to count. We all want to matter. Unfortunately, we often convince ourselves that subordinating others will allow us to count and matter more. The sense of superiority we feel when we put others down is pure self-deception.

Key concept: No person living in a prison of prejudice can be truly happy or free.[25]

Key questions: What individual or group are you having a hard time including even if they are doing you no real harm? Why?

Key Concepts

- The choice to include another human being activates our humanity.
- We include naturally in childhood and exclude unnaturally in adulthood.
- Including another human being should be an act of prejudgment based on that person's worth, not an act of judgment based on that person's worthiness.
- Instead of granting inclusion safety based on human status, we tend to judge another person's worthiness based on indicators like appearance, social status, or material possessions, when those indicators have nothing to do with worthiness.
- God may have made us of different clay, but there are no grounds to say that your clay is better than mine.
- In any social unit, inclusion safety can be granted, withheld, revoked, or partially or conditionally granted.
- We like to tell ourselves soothing stories to justify our sense of superiority.
- Excluding a person is more often the result of personal unmet needs and insecurities than a genuine dislike of the person.
- You learn inclusion when you practice inclusion. Behave until you believe.
- As you love people with action, you come to love them with emotion.
- No person living in a prison of prejudice can be truly happy or free.

Key Questions

- Do you treat people that you consider of lower status differently than those of higher status? If so, why?
- In the arc of every life are times when inclusion safety makes all the difference, when someone reaches out to include you at a vulnerable time. When did this happen to you? What impact did it have on your life? Are you paying it forward?
- How do you acknowledge and show sensitivity and appreciation for the cultural differences that exist on your team?
- Do you feel superior to other people? If so, why?
- Is the moral principle of inclusion a convenient or inconvenient truth for you?
- The basic social unit of the family is the primary laboratory for gaining a true civic education in inclusion safety. Did you learn it in your family? If not, do you intend to be a transformational figure in your family and model inclusion safety for the next generation?
- What conscious bias do you have? Ask a trusted friend where you may have unconscious bias. Finally, where do you exercise soft forms of exclusion to maintain barriers?
- What individual or group are you having a hard time including even if they are doing you no real harm? Why?

STAGE 2

Learner Safety

Real learning comes about when
the competitive spirit has ceased.
—Jiddu Krishnamurti

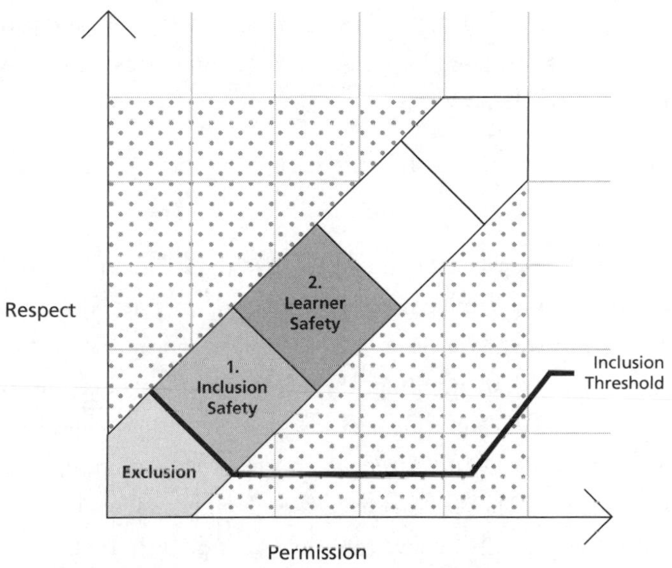

Figure 6. The second stage on the path to inclusion and innovation

The Human Need to Learn and Grow

In the second stage of psychological safety, we shift our focus from human status to human need—in this case the innate human need to learn and grow, to engage in all aspects of the learning process without fear of being rejected or neglected (figure 6, previous page).

Consider that in the United States of America, a student drops out of high school every twenty-six seconds.[1] Do we seriously believe these students are dropping out because they don't have the mental bandwidth to do the work? Except for those who may suffer from a legitimate learning disability, most of these students have ample ability to learn, graduate, and succeed in all aspects of personal and professional life. Most drop out because they fall behind, lack parental support at home, and find an apathetic learning environment at school.[2]

> **Key concept:** The true definition of devastation is no one caring when you fail.

Researchers have called the nearly two thousand high schools in America that suffer from chronically high dropout rates "dropout factories."[3] When we take a closer look at these schools, we see a pattern a neglect. More than anything, these failing students become emotionally estranged. Over time they lose confidence, feel defeated, and then call it quits. The indifference and lack of validation hijack their sense of identity. The fear that overtakes them grows from the inside out until they literally believe that they can't do it. In their forsaken condition, no one comes to their rescue.

> **Key concept:** In almost every case, parents and schools fail students before the students fail themselves.

> **Key question:** How many students do you know who flourish academically while they suffer emotionally?

There are three patterns of fear-inducing emotional danger that remove learner safety and create a state of risk: (1) neglect, (2) manipulation, and (3) coercion. Failing schools and classrooms tend to exhibit the first pattern of neglect. How about the workplace? When employees disengage and retreat into silence, they are often responding to a hostile and abusive environment. Fear comes as a result of ridicule, bullying, harassment, threats, and intimidation. These fear-inducing behaviors tend to conform to a pattern of manipulation and coercion.

I recently spent a day with a silent team. I've worked many teams and have come to learn that unnatural silence is usually an indication that a team has been neutralized by its leader. In this case, we were doing some long-range planning, but no one would speak up. The self-censoring instinct dominated the room, which is a sign that people are managing personal risk out of fear. The team had just failed on a big project and its members were suffering the period effects of that experience. But it wasn't the failure that stung, it was the leader's scorn that iced the team. Going silent is a normal response to being rejected, humiliated, or punished in some way. Silent team members disengage because they have no voice.

The alarming thing is when the abuse is tolerated. The leader of this team was emotionally disfiguring people, and no one would unmask the fiction that this guy's behavior was acceptable. He was nothing short of an equal opportunity harasser. I had a sidebar conversation with one of the team members after the meeting and asked her if the leader always acted this way. She confirmed that he did. Seeing an opportunity to discuss power dynamics, I asked, "Why do you put up with it?" Then came the reply, "We've just gotten used to it."

Key concept: While the unsafe school is most likely a nursery of neglect, the unsafe workplace is most likely a refuge of ridicule.

When it comes to low psychological safety, the failing school doesn't care about individuals or their performance. The failing workplace doesn't care about individuals either but does have a stake in their performance. Both are harmful, but in different ways. Finally, emotionally unsafe families demonstrate behaviors across the spectrum.

We see neglect in some, manipulation in others, and raw coercion in the most unhappy cases.

Key concept: A hostile learning environment, whether at home, school, or work, is a place where fear elicits the self-censoring instinct and shuts down the learning process.

In a fear-based classroom, defeated students drop out and confident students keep their heads down. Same story in the workplace: Top talent leaves because they have options. Mediocre talent stays because they don't. Meanwhile, productivity suffers. Finally, in an emotionally dysfunctional family, regardless of the pattern of that dysfunction, children wilt emotionally and tend to crumble academically.

Key concept: When the environment punishes rather than teaches, whether through neglect, manipulation, or coercion, individuals become more defensive, less reflective, and less able to self-diagnose, self-coach, and self-correct. That introduces the risk of real failure—the failure to keep trying.

Where learner safety exists, the leader creates a learning process with low social friction and low emotional expense. That requires levels of respect and permission that go beyond inclusion safety because the learning process itself introduces more risk, more vulnerability, and more potential exposure to social and emotional harm.

With inclusion safety, there's no active participation requirement other than to be humane and courteous, but with learner safety you must put yourself out there to ask questions, solicit feedback, float ideas, experiment, make mistakes, and even fail. You naturally look around and do a risk/reward calculation in your head: "If I ask that question, or request help, or make a suggestion, or admit I don't know, or make a mistake, what will it cost me? Can I be myself? Will I look stupid? Am I on trial? Will people laugh? Will they ignore me? Will I hurt my prospects? Will I damage my reputation?" In every learning context, consciously or not, we assess the level of interpersonal risk around us.

Table 2 adds the definition of respect and permission, as well as the social exchange requirement, for learner safety.

Table 2 **Stage 2 Learner Safety**

Stage	Definition of Respect	Definition of Permission	Social Exchange
1. Inclusion safety	Respect for the individual's humanity	Permission for the individual to interact with you as a human being	Inclusion in exchange for human status and the absence of harm
2. Learner safety	Respect for the individual's innate need to learn and grow	Permission for the individual to engage in all aspects of the learning process	Encouragement to learn in exchange for engagement in the learning process

To the universal need to be acknowledged, we add the universal need to learn and grow. Permission in this case is permission for the individual to engage in all aspects of the learning process. Inclusion safety requires that we show courtesy to each other, but with learner safety, we add another social exchange. If I'm giving learner safety to an individual, I want and expect the individual to make an effort to learn. If I'm the learner, I expect the leader, teacher, coach, or parent to support me in the learning process. It's encouragement to learn in exchange for engagement to learn.

Key concept: The moral imperative to grant learner safety is to act first by encouraging the learner to learn. Be the first mover.

Yes, learners must do their part to engage in the learning process, but sometimes they don't know how or have the confidence to try.

Individuals are often unprepared or unable to give the effort that learning requires. They don't believe they can learn and may be paralyzed from previous failures or embarrassments. In this case, we can't expect the learners to initiate the effort to learn when experience may have taught them that the risk is too great.

If you were to walk into the average classroom in a struggling high school, and we put you in charge of the class, what would you expect of the students? Engagement, energy, focus, confidence, self-efficacy? No, you would start with hope! We need to remind ourselves that we don't command learning, we invite it. The climate we create feeds the desire and motivation to learn. In an ideal setting, learner safety is a mutual giving and receiving of ideas, observations, questions, and discussion. If leaders are to meet learners where they are, you may need to back up and begin by supplying the inclusion safety that's been absent. I have yet to see learner safety where inclusion safety is absent. One builds on the other.

> **Key question:** Have you ever had a teacher that had more confidence in your ability to learn than you did? How did that influence your motivation and effort?

Let me emphasize that granting learner safety is not a passive act. When we grant it, we make a commitment to create a supportive and encouraging environment. We commit to be patient with learners. We commit to model effective learning, and we commit to share power, credit, and resources to enable all to learn. The learner's side of the social contract is different. The learner hopes, if not expects, to find a supportive and encouraging environment but commits to nothing up front because learning is a process fraught with personal risk. Learners rarely put forth the effort to learn unless learner safety is in place. It's a "build it and they will come" principle. If you don't build it, they may still come, but they won't learn.

Disconnecting Fear from Mistakes and Failure

If you walk into the high school gym at Lone Peak High School in Highland, Utah, on the second Saturday in May, you will see an ocean of chairs. The gym has been transformed into a giant classroom and more than three hundred students are sitting for the national Advanced Placement (AP) Calculus exam. Consider the irony: If you scan the high school academic landscape, the tallest peak—the Everest of them all—is calculus. And yet despite the fear factor, student demand for calculus has soared at this school. Why is there such an appetite for this challenging course?

The culprit is Craig B. Smith, a reformed electrical engineer who found his way to the classroom in 2007 after a highly successful career with ExxonMobil and other commercial organizations.[4] Craig teaches seven straight periods of calculus with an average class size of thirty-four. I have spent several hours interviewing Craig and his students and observing his classroom. Instead of meeting a jaded educator surrendered to the woes of American secondary education, you will find a man brimming with enthusiasm for his students and his craft. Officially, Craig teaches calculus. Unofficially, he presides over a leadership laboratory as a coach, grief counselor, and triage nurse. A true outlier, Craig is widely regarded as one of the best secondary math teachers in the nation. Judging from normalized data taken from the Utah State Office of Education, he may be the best.

In 2006, the year before Craig began teaching calculus, 46 students per thousand took the AP Calculus AB test at Lone Peak High School. Eight years later in 2016, 160 students per thousand took the AB test (a nearly 250 percent jump), compared to 34 students per thousand statewide. The current participation rate is 800 percent higher than the national average. What about performance? In 2006, 13 students per thousand at Lone Peak passed the standardized AP Calculus AB exam administered by the College Board, compared to a little higher rate of 22 per thousand among students throughout the state. In 2014, the state pass rate per thousand was still stuck at 22, whereas the pass rate for Craig's students rocketed to 114 per thousand, a stunning 777 percent increase. It's one thing to make steady incremental improvement. It's quite another to engineer a radical transformation. In an era when American teenagers don't even crack the global top 20 among developed nations in math performance, Craig's achievements are stunning.

He begins with one all-important preconception, one rigid bias, one unyielding prejudice: that every student can learn calculus. His math dojo is a personal development center that rejects the idea that learning ability is fixed or implanted at birth.[5] "I try never to judge a student's aptitude or effort." Craig maintains that slow students are not less intelligent students. They simply assimilate at a slower pace, so his focus is on student effort rather than aptitude. That ability to resist making discriminating judgments of students' abilities is a skill, but it's also a moral capacity, and one that many teachers don't have the discipline to develop. Many teachers make aptitude judgments and begin sorting and assigning value to their students immediately. As the Nobel Prize–winning researcher Daniel Kahneman observes, "You tend to form a global impression unless you make a special effort not to form a global impression."[6] Craig began suppressing that natural impulse years ago.

> **Key question:** When you start working with new people, do you judge their aptitude immediately or do you suppress that impulse?

Harvard Business School's legendary C. Roland Christensen echoed the same conclusion:

> I believe in the unlimited potential of every student. At first glance they range, like instructors, from mediocre to magnificent. But potential is invisible to the superficial gaze. It takes faith to discern it, but I have witnessed too many academic

> miracles to doubt its existence. I now view each student as "material for a work of art." If I have faith, deep faith, in students' capacities for creativity and growth, how very much we can accomplish together. If, on the other hand, I fail to believe in that potential, my failure sows seeds of doubt. Students read our negative signals, however carefully cloaked, and retreat from creative risk to the "just possible." When this happens, everyone loses.[7]

In social psychology, there's a vein of research devoted to what is called stereotype threat theory, which says that when we are subjected to a negative stereotype, we tend to conform to it. In other words, labels limit. They can also enlarge and magnify. With negative stereotypes, simply being aware that you may be part of one can motivate us to conform to the invisible limitation. Stereotypes about race, gender, age, body image, and learning ability can exert significant psychic damage on their targets. As Claude Steele notes, stereotype threat can result in "low self-esteem, low expectations, low motivation, self-doubt."[8]

Key concept: Expectations shape behavior in both directions. When you set the bar high or low, people tend to jump high or low.

Stereotypes can also influence individuals to stretch to higher levels of performance. Craig helps students shed any psychic damage a harmful stereotype may be inflicting. Every year students arrive with the conviction that they are poor at math, and every year those same students pass the national AP Calculus exam.

To the belief that everyone can learn calculus, Craig adds the precondition of learner safety. As he explains it, "I can't teach students unless I like them. I can't like them unless I know them, and I can't know them unless I talk to them." That's why he spends the first class period every term doing nothing but learning his students' names and a little about their lives. After that, everyone gets down to work, but he continues to punctuate his class time with short, personal touch points with each student. He begins each class by checking in with each student to acknowledge him or her individually and to check on homework completion.

In my classroom observations, I notice that Craig toggles back and forth between lecture and discussion.[9] The choreography seems effortless, creating a feeling of relaxed intensity and a total absence of fear, inhibition, or formality. Craig teaches a concept in lecture style and then asks a series of questions in discussion style to test understanding. He uses a participation point system that reinforces questions as the students navigate through an emotional and intellectual journey of small victories and defeats. "A wrong answer is as good as a right answer, as long as you know why," he maintains.

Key concept: Failure isn't the exception, it's the expectation and the way forward. There will be discouragement before discovery.

Indeed, if you're really trying, there should be no stigma, no shame, and no embarrassment associated with failure. It's simply a stepping-stone. We should reward failure because it's not failure; it's progress. The examination of failure is often more valuable than the examination of success. Consistent with this principle, Craig has debunked the conventional wisdom that test retakes—the practice of allowing students to retake a test if they do poorly—don't work. "It's a little more work for the teacher," Craig observes. "Retesting clearly works, so I give endless chances. If you're willing to work, there's always mercy. You can try again."

Craig invites students to learn without adding fear to a subject that already creates its own. He recognizes that students who are emotionally distressed—anxious, angry, or depressed—are cognitively impaired and don't learn well, so he fosters a challenging and yet nurturing climate of learner safety to dramatically reduce learning risk. "There's no embarrassment in Mr. Smith's class," one student said. "You never feel dumb even if you don't understand something."

Key question: Does your team punish failure? Do you punish failure?

Learner safety requires low ego and uncommonly high emotional intelligence, traits that Craig possesses in abundance. He's a man of great warmth who clearly seeks to bless rather than impress his students. He's not competitive, combative, or punitive. He's not there to pontificate, display brilliance, or duel with his students. Instead, he shows patience and intellectual humility. Perhaps what is most invisible of all is the way he monitors both content and context. He has developed an acute social sensitivity to interpret the nonverbal cues of the students. He is fluent in this language, which allows him to stay in sync with the students' cognitive and emotional progress so that he never runs past them.[10]

"He never acts bothered or irritated when you ask a question," another student said. "He'll kneel down by your desk, find out what you know, and help you from there. But he doesn't give you the answer. You have to explain where and why you're stuck."

Key question: Do you learn as much or more from your failures as your successes?

"Calculus is not an easy subject," Craig says. "I also recognize that many of my students will never use calculus again. What we're trying to do is build confident, self-reliant, mentally tenacious, and unafraid students who are prepared for life. The journey makes you accountable. It makes you stretch. It makes you feel good about yourself. Yes, I teach calculus. More importantly, I teach students."

Does Craig understand calculus better than other calculus teachers? Is this the source of his competitive advantage? Clearly not. Based on his extraordinary perceptive capacity and ability to ward off compassion fatigue, he has mastered the art of shaping the social, emotional, and cognitive context, in creating a figuratively "clean, well-lighted place" where the whole student can flourish.[11] This is learner safety.

The Intellectual and the Emotional

A person's ability to learn requires staying focused, managing impulses, and avoiding distractions. Researchers use terms such as *flow state*, *meta-cognition*, *executive function*, *effective effort*, and *high engagement* to describe what good learners do. These terms refer to the supervisory attentional or cognitive control system.

If we have learned anything about learning, we've learned that it's not an isolated, rational process that is cold, dry, and mechanistic. Emotion is nested in reason, and reason in emotion. Cognition and affect are inseparably connected. Before I went to Oxford, I earned a master's degree at the University of Utah. My adviser was an internationally respected political scientist named John Francis. He helped prepared me academically for Oxford by spilling red ink all over my papers. He pushed me, stretched me, and roughed me up. In one class, I became absolutely exasperated because I could never earn an A on a paper. I'd sit down with John in his office and go over his corrections, and every time I'd walk away with lingering frustration, yet loving this man. There was a beautiful weirdness about the process that motivated me to redouble my efforts. He was driving me crazy, but I wasn't disengaging. As he connected with me personally, I gave him permission to push me.

> **Key question:** Have you had a teacher in your life that created learner safety and pushed you to a new level of performance?

And what did he do in the classroom? He shared power through discussion. He's a brilliant man, but there was little didactic and zero pedantic time in his courses. A traditional lecture is authoritarian. John opted for a more democratic and collaborative approach where we learned together. This of course created more risk for the students because we bore more responsibility to teach each other, but out of that joint ownership came a deeper emotional investment and a greater willingness to take risks in the learning process.

A leader can maintain a culture of learning only if he or she consistently minimizes vulnerability through a consistent pattern of positive emotional response.[12] People want to see how you react to dissent and bad news. If you listen intently, respond constructively, and convey appreciation, participants absorb these cues and calculate their participation accordingly.

Key concept: The most important signal in granting or withholding learner safety is the leader's emotional response to dissent and bad news.

As a teacher, John had mastered the integration of cognitive and affective systems. If you lose emotional engagement, intellectual engagement slows down or may not happen at all. People learn from the people they love more than from the people they don't.

Key concept: Humans process socially, emotionally, and intellectually at the same time.

Learning is not the operation of a detached, dispassionate data center; it's an interplay of the head and the heart. Another witness, and perhaps our biggest proof source for the need for learner safety, is the internet, educational technology, and the democratization of learning. The barriers to learning that have stood resolutely for millennia are coming down. The infinite scalability of the internet allows anyone access to the best content and the best teachers in the world. All you need is a smart device and internet access. As the traditional barriers of access, cost, and quality fall, we should theoretically see a surge in learning across all populations. My daughter can go to Kahn Academy for help with linear algebra; my son can watch a brief TED-Ed video on the history of cheese; and I can go to edX to watch Michael Sandel teach a course on justice. It costs nothing and it's on demand.

With the internet, you can learn anything you want, anytime you want, anyplace you want. It's the great equalizer, except for one thing: you need focus and motivation, and therein lies the problem. We have entered a time of unprecedented opportunity for human improvement, when the challenge is no longer time and access, but desire and discipline. Educational technology has created a learning renaissance, but it's leaving millions behind who lack the interest, confidence, and drive to participate, largely because they've been deprived of learner safety.

Humans learn in context, not in isolation, and they are continuously influenced by that context. When the learning context is encouraging, it taps the drive to be curious. Add to that the fact that the level of learner safety directly shapes the way learners interact. "The degree and quality of learner participation in interprofessional simulation courses," writes the Dutch social scientist Babette Bronkhorst, "is influenced by self-efficacy as well as perceptions of the psychological safety of the learning environment. Learners who feel safe are far more willing to practice at the edge of their expertise to experiment, solve difficult problems, and to reflect on their performance."[13]

Learner safety is an enabling precondition that creates the curiosity and willingness to be brave in personal learning. Bill Gates said, "People who are as curious as I am will be fine in any system. For the self-motivated student, these are the golden days. I wish I was growing up now. I envy my son. If he and I are talking about something that we don't understand, we just watch videos and click on articles, and that feeds our discussion. Unfortunately, the highly curious student is a small percentage of the kids."[14]

Gates says that only a small percentage of kids are highly curious but notice what he does with his own son. He gets knee to knee and shoulder to shoulder and they learn together. He makes an emotional connection with his son to fuel intellectual exploration. It's amazing how quickly the curiosity and motivation to learn can be kindled when someone creates the nurturing environment of learner safety.

Key question: When was the last time you created a nurturing learning environment for another person's curiosity and motivation?

Remember that humans instinctively look for learner safety before they engage in the learning process. If you know you're going to be ridiculed if you ask a question, the self-censoring instinct will hush that impulse and transition you to a defensive routine. Trusted leaders have security clearance. Distrusted leaders are barred entry. When it comes to learner safety, the learner has the final say.

Key concept: We guard our social and emotional selves with sophisticated personal surveillance systems.

From Tonga to Philadelphia

Consider the story of my college football teammate Vai Sikahema. His family arrived on American soil from the island nation of Tonga when he was eight years old. They settled in Mesa, Arizona, where Vai's father found work as a janitor. With no English-language programs available at his school, Vai sat in the back of class, listening but not understanding.

"I felt so vulnerable and threatened," he said, "that I wouldn't admit that English was my second language. I was embarrassed by my culture, my language, and even my name. I just wanted a regular name that people could pronounce and wouldn't make fun of. And you have to understand, I was just getting used to wearing shoes."

Vai gravitated to sports such as boxing and football, where his physical gifts brought immediate rewards and defined a path for his social and cultural integration. His parents provided a loving environment, but with limited education themselves and no experience to support him academically, Vai fell seriously behind. Because formal education was uncharted territory, Vai's parents deferred to his high school coaches, who directed him toward athletic scholarships, giving little more than a nod to his studies. Consequently, Vai took most of his high school classes from coaches and carried the high aspiration of maintaining a 2.0 grade point average to keep his eligibility to play football.

As each year passed, the academic gap widened, except in one subject—English. Vai had a high school English teacher named Barbara Nielsen. After observing Vai in her class, she immediately noticed his reading, writing, and speaking deficiencies. At age fifteen, he was reading at a fifth-grade level, five years behind his peers. Barbara called Vai's parents and arranged to come to their home every Saturday to practice reading. And she didn't stop there: She put Vai on the student newspaper staff, where he eventually developed facility with the English language and learned to write articles. Week after week, she would come to the house and they would slog through *Great Expectations* and *To Kill a Mockingbird*. Vai would read and Barbara would ask him questions. He didn't know it at the time, but the learner safety Barbara created would become a solacing influence and a pivot of change in his life that would sustain his future learning efforts in the years to come.

Vai had a five-year learning gap in reading comprehension at age fifteen, but he had a much larger gap in math and science. That gap never closed. Meanwhile, he excelled in football and accepted a full-ride NCAA scholarship to Brigham Young University. Vai studied hard, but grit alone could not close the massive learning gap in math and science.

Key concept: Grit alone will not close a learning gap. Learner safety is essential.

After flunking his Physical Science 101 class and doing poorly in other classes, he started to lose confidence. Eventually, he wrote off the possibility of earning a college degree. Instead, he focused on staying eligible to play football by taking a variety of entry-level courses. Before he left BYU, he flunked Physical Science five times and never declared a major course of study. As he put it, "I was just trying to hang on."

Vai went on to become the first Tongan American to play in the National Football League, playing on three teams during eight seasons and being twice named to the Pro Bowl as a punt returner. Fast-forward eight years. Vai retires from the NFL and is hired at WCAU, the CBS-owned television station in Philadelphia, to do weekend sports. The station is later sold to NBC, and Vai eventually moves to weekdays and then becomes a morning news anchor and the station's sports director. An NFL pedigree was a nice thing to have, but where and how did Vai learn broadcast journalism, and what gave him the courage to try? The little-known secret is what Vai chose to do during his off-season. He would go to the local television station and ask to work as an intern. "I learned to make coffee, get doughnuts, and tear scripts. They gave me small opportunities to work on my diction. I had to show people that I'm not above rolling up my sleeves and doing things pro athletes wouldn't normally do."

Vai far outlasted the average NFL career of 3.3 years but knew it would come to an end. With four kids and no degree, he also knew that he had to do something to prepare for the future. "I had many mentors along the way, but I have to tell you that much of the motivation to learn this business goes all the way back to Mrs. Nielsen. She planted a seed in me when I was fifteen, and it never died." To tie a bow on his unlikely journey, Vai enrolled at a local community college in Philadelphia and earned an A in Physical Science 101.

"There is *no* relation," Stanford's Carol Dweck maintains, "between students' abilities or intelligence and the development of mastery-oriented qualities. Some of the very brightest students avoid challenges, dislike effort, and wilt in the face of difficulty. And some of the less bright students are real go-getters, thriving on challenge, persisting intensely when things get difficult, and accomplishing more than you expected."[15] What Dweck doesn't mention is the crucial role the environment plays in all of this. Thus, the social exchange of encouragement for engagement that defines learner safety. I can't say that I know a single person who has overcome the adversities of life without some help. There's always someone who plays a pivotal role as Mrs. Nielsen did for Vai. In this case, she planted her influence early, and that influence emboldened him to be almost indifferent to failure. A moment's reflection reveals that the true formula for success is to work hard and get help. And where an individual begins life's journey with disadvantages, learner safety can become the great equalizer.

> **Key question:** Can you think of a person that played a pivotal role in your life by creating learner safety and believed in your ability to learn?

Decommoditizing People in Organizations

The management ranks of many organizations are still populated by baby boomers who are barely hanging on, trying to avoid career misfortune until retirement, clinging to old skills from another time, immobilized, publicly acknowledging the new world but privately unwilling to learn in it.

Why are they doing this? They fell behind and now they're caught between two worlds. They grew up in a world that obsessed on the machines that provided automation, mass production, and economies of scale and didn't pay much attention to human capital, especially their own.

Human capital is everything. And yet, Steve Kerr, the first person to wear the title of chief learning officer, was appointed to that position at General Electric by then CEO Jack Welch in 1994. The acknowledgment of the individual as the source of productive capacity was a slow, evolutionary process. The prevailing mindset held that only a small part of an organization's population could learn and contribute as knowledge workers. Leaders operated on the assumption that there were thinking and nonthinking parts of the organization. Influenced by the work of Frederick Winslow Taylor, organizations restricted and compartmentalized human labor as measured in terms of raw task-based productivity. The larger nonthinking part of the organization was not even considered for its creative output, a mindset mired in centuries of prejudice that made us blind to people's potential.

Key concept: The prejudiced mind is willfully blind.

Even within the thinking part of the organization, the mindset emphasized onetime learning for permanent qualification. This inherited model from the industrial age rested on a basic tenet that valued assets and commoditized people. Despite organizational behaviorists appearing on the scene in the latter part of the twentieth century, the legacy of hierarchy and the rules-based emphasis on accountability and internal control remained the focus.

Think about that legacy in today's context. The natural rise and fall of competitive advantage is nothing new. What is new is the average length of that rise and fall. It's much shorter. As that trend continues, learning becomes more important to success because the half-life of an organization's knowledge mirrors its competitive strategy. An overall compression of timeframes naturally shifts the source of ongoing competitiveness to learning. A competitive cycle is a learning cycle. Either learn and retool to maintain competitiveness or face the grave risk of irrelevance.

We used to think of learning as discrete and event-based, something that was triggered by a problem or question. Now it's continuous and embedded in workflow. As a result, it's becoming increasingly difficult to separate learning from production because of the interwoven nature of acquiring knowledge and creating value. The boundary between the two processes is thinner than ever as individuals toggle back and forth in real time. Process technologies will eventually integrate with learning and talent-management systems to facilitate a more seamless integration of workflow and learning.

The danger is to believe that technology is the secret sauce that can set you free in your quest to be a learning organization. This overabundant faith in the power of technology is what Richard Florida refers to as "techno-utopianism."[16] Impressive as the advances in collaborative technology are, they can't overcome the formidable barrier of fear that autocratic leadership always plants. And yet we continue to hear evangelists proclaiming the limitless potential of the latest technology advances such as mash-up web applications, virtual-learning worlds, hackathons, and performance-support tools. The technology-hype cycle, romanticism, and offers of salvation never go away.

It's helpful to reflect on what an organization really is. There are many definitions, but perhaps the best one for our time was put forward by the education theorist Malcolm Knowles. He invites us to think of an organization as a "system of learning as well as production."[17] In our day, organizations literally compete based on their ability to learn. In an unforgiving, hypercompetitive environment, creating an organization that learns at or above the speed of change—the very definition of learning agility—is the central organizational challenge of our time.

Peter Drucker coined the term *knowledge worker* in 1959, and yet we're still trying to break down industrial age orthodoxies. We continue to elevate hard-core authoritarian bosses, conditioned in another time and place, to lead organizations. The only reason they survive is that their organizations have sources of competitive advantage that compensate for and conceal their liabilities. The increasing demands of a protean organization require a leader to be direction setter, servant, coach, enabler, and facilitator. We see the predominant patterns of leadership continuing their migration from bureaucratic and autocratic to democratic and egalitarian, from task oriented to people oriented, and from directive to facilitative.

Not only is this a fundamental change from the leader-as-oracle model, but it also requires leaders to assume a very different emotional and social posture. Leaders must become comfortable portraying themselves as competent through their ability to learn and adapt rather than their expertise. To foster learner safety, leaders must model a level of humility and curiosity that is simply alien to most traditional conceptions of leadership. Ironically, leaders are being challenged to develop confidence in the very act of not knowing. They must be submissive to the fact that they will pass through periods of temporary incompetence as they move through learning cycles.

As one who has worked with some very difficult teams, I want to offer two final suggestions to cultivate and preserve learner safety. First, manage those who learn with their mouths—the vocally aggressive members of your team who are prone to menace their colleagues with verbal firestorms and shafts of criticism. Second, never let hierarchy relieve anyone of the responsibility to learn. When I train executive teams, about half the CEOs don't attend. The others come eager to learn. Who has the advantage?

> **Key questions:** Do you model the leader as learner or the leader as oracle? Do you demonstrate an aggressive, self-directed learning disposition?

Leaders committed to safeguard learner safety understand that learning is where competitive advantage comes from, that it represents the highest form of enterprise risk management, and that the biggest risk a firm can take is to cease to learn. It seems increasingly clear that leaders who do not demonstrate deep patterns of aggressive and self-directed learning in their own disposition are almost certain to fail. Those who do are almost certain to succeed, provided, they combine those learning patterns with the ability to engage people. Ultimately, learner safety doesn't happen unless it is modeled, communicated, taught, measured, recognized, and rewarded.

> **Key question:** How can you remove the barrier of learner anxiety to the point that the most inhibited and fearful member of the team will come forward and engage?

Your team may be exquisitely endowed with brilliant people and abundant resources, but if individuals don't feel free to probe, prod, poke, pilot, and prototype, ask silly questions, stretch and stumble, they won't venture.[18] Learner safety is important because it encourages these specific learning behaviors. What's even more impressive is that it can act as an invisible leveling agent to remove the hesitation and reduce the anxiety employees often feel in asking for help from those who could literally terminate their employment.[19] In the end, we each have a choice to cultivate or crush, nurture or neglect, stimulate or stifle learner safety.

Key Concepts

- The true definition of devastation is no one caring when you fail.
- In almost every case, parents and schools fail students before the students fail themselves.
- While the unsafe school is most likely a nursery of neglect, the unsafe workplace is most likely a refuge of ridicule.
- A hostile learning environment, whether at home, school, or work, is a place where fear elicits the self-censoring instinct and shuts down the learning process.
- When the environment punishes rather than teaches, whether through neglect, manipulation, or coercion, we become more defensive, less reflective, and less able to self-diagnose, self-coach, and self-correct. That opens people up to the risk of real failure—the failure to keep trying.
- The moral imperative to grant learner safety is to act first by encouraging the learner to learn. Be the first mover.
- Expectations shape behavior in both directions. When you set the bar high or low, people tend to jump high or low.
- Failure isn't the exception, it's the expectation and the way forward.
- Humans process socially, emotionally, and intellectually at the same time.
- The most important signal in granting or withholding learner safety is the leader's emotional response to dissent and bad news.

- We guard our social and emotional selves with sophisticated personal surveillance systems.
- Grit alone will not close a learning gap. You also need learner safety.
- The prejudiced mind is willfully blind.

Key Questions

- How many students do you know who flourish academically while they suffer emotionally?
- Have you ever had a teacher that had more confidence in your ability to learn than you did? How did that influence your motivation and effort?
- When you start working with new people, do you judge their aptitude immediately or do you suppress that impulse?
- Does your team punish failure? Do you punish failure?
- Do you learn as much or more from your failures as your successes?
- Have you had a teacher in your life that created learner safety and pushed you to a new level of performance?
- When was the last time you created a nurturing learning environment for another person's curiosity and motivation?
- Can you think of a person that played a pivotal role in your life by creating learner safety and believed in your ability to learn?
- How can you lower the barrier of learner anxiety to the point that the most inhibited and fearful member of the team will come forward and engage?
- Do you model the leader as learner or the leader as oracle? Do you demonstrate an aggressive, self-directed learning disposition?

STAGE 3

Contributor Safety

"I look upon ourselves as partners in all of this, and that each of us contributes and does what he can do best. And so I see not a top rung and a bottom rung—I see all this horizontally—and I see this as part of a matrix."

—Jonas Salk

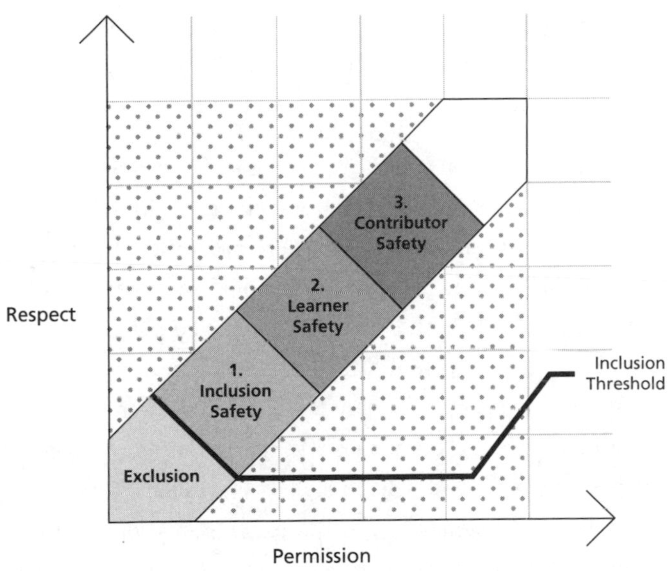

Figure 7. The third stage on the path to inclusion and innovation

A Signal That It's Go Time!

Have you ever been on an athletic team but didn't get to play in the games? Instead, you sat the bench. What does it feel like to ride the pine? If your teammates accepted you, you had member safety. If you practiced hard, you had learner safety. But if you never played in the games, you didn't have contributor safety (figure 7, previous page).

Sitting the bench is a state of suspension between preparation and performance. It's socially and emotionally painful. Then one day the coach taps you on the shoulder and says, "Get in the game." In an instant, you're on the field. You're not spectating anymore, you're contributing. In that moment, satisfaction replaces suspension. You're no longer preparing for something that never comes.

> **Key concept:** Except for those who may be paralyzed by fear or anxiety, human beings have a deep and unrelenting drive to play in the game.

In stage 1, inclusion safety, we accept the individual on human grounds. In stage 2, learner safety, we encourage the individual's learning on human grounds as well, and then encourage that individual to engage in the learning process. But the next stage of psychological safety is not a natural right. Rather, it's an earned privilege based on demonstrated performance. With contributor safety, we provide autonomy in exchange for performance. We will empower you if you can deliver results. Contributor safety marks the end of the apprenticeship and the beginning of solid, self-directed performance. It's time to put something meaningful on the table. The leader grants contributor safety when the individual has the chops to do the job. In business terms, it means the individual is an asset rather than a liability, a net contributor delivering a positive return on investment. The organization grants respect and permission based on the individual's ability to create value.

Contributor safety makes greater demands on both parties. This is a mutual investment in which the individual invests effort and skill, and the team invests support, guidance, and direction. When the progression to contributor safety works, the team empowers the individual and says, "Go do it!" Similarly, the individual at this point is now prepared and has developed a greater desire to contribute, and says, "Let me do it." This is the current situation with my son, who recently received his driver's license. He passed the written test and the road test. His mother and I logged forty hours of daytime driving practice and eight hours of nighttime driving practice with him to meet the licensing requirements.

At this point, it would be quite unnatural for him to say to me, "Dad, can you drive me to my friend's house?" He wants to take the wheel. And that's as it should be.

Key concept: The preparation to perform creates the desire to perform.

That's why you can't be content riding the pine forever. The social exchange in this third stage is guided autonomy for performance. But if the individual doesn't perform, the organization retrenches to learner safety. Once you get in the game, you've got to carry your weight, or you'll soon be on the bench again. On the other hand, if you can contribute but never get the chance, you'll either decide to live with that reality or find another team.

Contributor safety is therefore the full activation of the social contract. Once the individual graduates from trainee status, he or she expects to be treated like a full-fledged member of the team, and the organization expects a meaningful contribution. If learner safety is the stage of preparation, contributor safety is the stage of performance. Crossing over to contributor safety is the signal that it's go time, that the team is trusting you to perform in the role it has given you. The organization is expecting you to carry your load and perform competently.

The basic unit of performance in the twenty-first century is the team. Chances are that you will participate as a member of numerous intact and cross-functional teams during your professional lifetime.

You will colocate with some and span the globe with others. In fact, as organizations get flatter, it's becoming more common to be a member of several teams at the same time.[1] Regardless of the nature of work you do and the team you're a part of, this third stage of psychological safety will always be the foundation of performance.

Execution versus Innovation

If learner safety fosters preparation and contributor safety fosters performance, what exactly do we mean by *performance*? Answer: execution and innovation.

> **Key concept:** Organizations engage in only two processes—execution and innovation. Execution is the creation and delivery of value today, while innovation is the creation and delivery of value tomorrow.

The differences in those two processes are fundamental. Execution is about economizing work and scaling processes. It's about control and driving out variability to achieve efficiency. Innovation is the opposite. It's about freedom, imagination, creativity, and the introduction of variability. Because execution is more about standardization, and innovation is more about deviation, there's a natural tension and tradeoff between the two. The fundamental distinction between execution and innovation is true whether you're a multinational corporation or the local chapter of the shiitake mushroom growers' association. Does that mean that contributor safety is solely about execution and not innovation? Not quite. This is where the progression of psychological safety gets even more interesting.

Innovation can be further divided into offensive and defensive types. Offensive innovation is proactive, while defensive innovation is reactive. Both are responses to adaptive challenges, just different kinds.

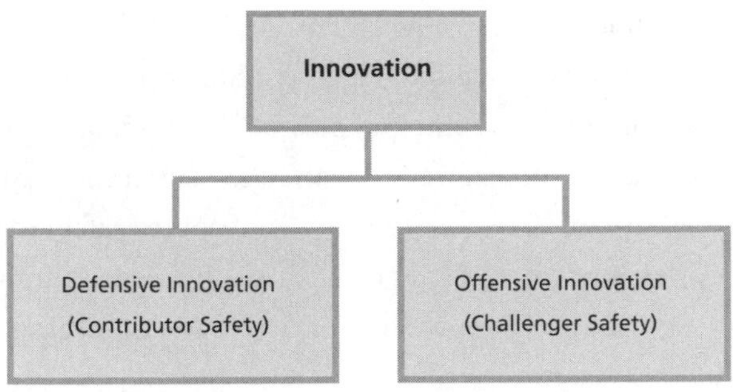

Figure 8. Defensive versus offensive innovation in stages 3 and 4

Key concept: Offensive innovation is a response to an opportunity, while defensive innovation is a response to a threat or crisis.

Offensive innovation is you choosing change. Defensive innovation is change choosing you. Why does the distinction matter? It matters because defensive innovation is a natural part of contributor safety, while offensive innovation is not. Figure 8 shows the two types graphically.

When I was the plant manager at Geneva Steel, we sold plate steel to Caterpillar. They used it to make parts for the large equipment they manufactured. At one point, they informed us that the surface quality of our plate steel was no longer acceptable. They were tightening their quality parameters and we could either figure out a way to meet them or they would find another supplier. So here we were, confronted with a new adaptive challenge. In this case, it was a threat quickly bordering on a crisis. I still remember calling our team together for the first emergency meeting. It was all hands on deck—the operators; the process, chemical, metallurgical, and quality engineers; the maintenance folks—all trying to figure out how to remove small surface-level defects. Not only did we need good root-cause analysis and corrective action, we needed defensive innovation and we needed it fast.

This example is typical of what happens in just about every organization. Stakeholder demands change, consumer preferences evolve, new competitors emerge, demographics shift, technology accelerates. We either engage in defensive innovation to stay in the game or we bow out because we don't have enough contributor safety to frankly discuss mistakes or improvements. The reason defensive innovation is part of contributor safety is that it's riskier to do nothing than to formulate a response.

> **Key principle:** When an external threat challenges the status quo, the natural fear of challenging the status quo is replaced with the survival instinct.

At this point, we want and expect defensive innovation. You're no longer taking a personal risk to challenge the status quo. You can thank an outside force for performing that task for you. In this case, it was Caterpillar, and once they issued the challenge, there was no fear associated with challenging the status quo. Survival was now at stake.

For nearly every team or organization that I've observed, this pattern holds true. Engaging in defensive innovation to survive is within the realm of normal expectations. You seldom feel threatened internally when you're threatened externally.

> **Key question:** Have you ever had an external threat that removed the fear of challenging the status quo?

In fact, external threats bind you together. They act as an agent of alignment, providing the clear and present danger of a common enemy. Proactive innovation, however, is another matter. It involves far more personal risk and thus a higher level of psychological safety based on higher levels of respect and permission. That, of course, is the preserve of challenger safety, which we will discuss in the next chapter. To summarize, then, contributor safety fosters execution and defensive innovation, but falls short of addressing the higher level of risk and vulnerability that is usually needed for offensive innovation.

Guided Autonomy in Exchange for Results

The social contract for the third stage of contributor safety trades autonomy for performance. The social unit grants the individual increased independence and ownership as he or she demonstrates the ability to contribute based not only on acquired knowledge and skills, but also on good work habits and disciplined follow-through—both know-how and reliability. In short, when we move to the contributor stage, we move to a higher level of individual accountability (table 3). Any individual who moves to the contributor stage is responsible for a work product, results, and deliverables. My teenage children have daily and weekly chores to complete, musical instruments to practice, homework to do, and dogs to feed. The higher the performance, the greater the autonomy.

Regardless of the individual's performance, we retain the moral responsibility to grant inclusion safety and learner safety, provided the

Table 3 Stage 3 Contributor Safety

Stage	Definition of Respect	Definition of Permission	Social Exchange
1. Inclusion safety	Respect for the individual's humanity	Permission for the individual to interact with you as a human being	Inclusion in exchange for human status and the absence of harm
2. Learner safety	Respect for the individual's innate need to learn and grow	Permission for the individual to engage in all aspects of the learning process	Encouragement in exchange for engagement
3. Contributor safety	Respect for the individual's ability to create value	Permission for the individual to work with independence and their own judgment	Guided autonomy in exchange for results

individual is courteous and willing to learn. The morality of contributor safety, however, is different because the individual bears a higher responsibility. Contributor safety is a mutual investment by the individual and the social unit, not a natural right, and not something human beings are entitled to by virtue of their human status. You must earn it, and it's an instinct for leaders to grant more autonomy as other human beings under their charge become more self-directed and deliver the expected results. My wife and I frequently remind our children that parenting is the gradual transfer of responsibility, and the sooner our children are willing to take it on, the sooner we are willing to give it.

> **Key concept:** When you're competent and willing to hold yourself accountable, you're ready to receive contributor safety.

With contributor safety, the organization assumes risk on behalf of the individual, who is expected to contribute. When something goes wrong, the liability associated with the risk of failure normally falls back on the organization rather than the individual. If my company's software development team delivers a bug-ridden solution to one of our customers, we all feel the pain. Not surprisingly, the higher the risk associated with performance, the less autonomy we grant, even if we have enormous trust in the individual, her skills, and her reliability. When I managed the steel plant, we had no fewer than ten thousand written standard operating procedures, governing every stage of the steel-making process.

If the organization grants contributor safety as it should, you can expect it when you earn it. This also means you will be denied it if you're not ready or fall seriously short. That's why we wait to see a track record of consistent performance before granting full contributor safety. In fact, if the individual isn't prepared to do a job, it would be foolish to offer contributor safety. We do it gradually based on performance to manage risk along the way.

Key question: Have you ever granted contributor safety too fast when the person either didn't have the skill or wasn't willing to assume responsibility for the results?

Making the Transition to Contribution

In many organizations, the transition to contributor safety corresponds with the completion of formal training and the earning of a credential that certifies that the individual is ready to perform a specific job, role, or function. For example, doctors, lawyers, teachers, engineers, airline pilots, brick masons, accountants, and sometimes even floral designers must pass certifying exams to demonstrate competence and be admitted as members of their professional societies. But there are even more roles that don't rely on formal credentialing and admittance—the golf pro, the TV news anchor, the Little League coach, the barista, and the surfing instructor. And then there are some roles where credentials are optional—the chef, the river guide, the landscaper, or the personal trainer. The transition from preparation to performance can be formal or informal, and it may come gradually or immediately (table 4).

Formal immediate. To become a lawyer requires three years of law school or apprenticeship, but you are authorized to practice law in a state only after you pass the bar exam in that state. The transition to

Table 4 **Ways of Transitioning from Preparation to Performance**

Formal Immediate (Lawyer)	**Formal Gradual** (Reporter)
Informal Immediate (Athlete)	**Informal Gradual** (Parent)

the stage of contribution is formal and immediate once you pass the exam. You're certainly not an experienced lawyer, but you have the minimum knowledge and skills to perform the role.

Formal gradual. Examples of formal gradual transitions to performance are less common because a formal process implies an event or measurement of some kind to identify the change. A formal gradual transition usually involves a qualitative rather than a quantitative judgment of the individual's capacity to do a job. For instance, I worked with a newspaper that hired a new journalist to write stories. The hiring and appointment to the role of reporter was formal, but that reporter was initially considered a cub reporter in the learning stage. The transition to become a feature writer and take on in-depth stories was a gradual process supervised by the managing editor. There was no test or certification, but rather a slow transition based on the maturing reporting ability of the individual. Many jobs in the business world are like this: you are appointed to a job, but a big skills gap still has to be closed before you can contribute competently in the role.

Informal immediate. An informal immediate move to performance is one in which there is no formal credentialing or appointment to accompany the transition. This often happens when needs arise in real time because of a shortage or a surge in demand. Someone needs to step in and fill the need. For example, an athlete gets injured and her replacement is called into the game immediately. An employee unexpectedly leaves an organization and you're asked to lead the team.

Informal gradual. Finally, an informal and gradual transition to contribution is perhaps the most common pattern of all. It represents the natural process of maturing into higher performance. The most important roles that I have in life are that of husband and father. Ironically, in these most crucial responsibilities, I'm not formally credentialed, licensed, or certified. Now it's true that the day of my marriage marked the day I became a husband, but it didn't qualify me to become one. Similarly, I formally became a father the moment my son was born, but again, the event of his birth did not coincide with my competent performance as a father. Having the role doesn't mean you can perform in the role. In both cases, I had much to learn. I assumed these roles before I was adequately prepared for them. But isn't that true with most roles, positions, and assignments in life? Don't we often have to grow into them?

Three Levels of Accountability

The autonomy-for-results exchange that defines contributor safety is an exchange that increases in scale and scope as the individual learns to contribute more. The granting of contributor safety follows a consistent pattern in which the social unit gives autonomy based on three levels of accountability—task, process, and outcome (table 5).

Table 5 **The Three Levels of Accountability**

3. Outcome
2. Process
1. Task

If we consistently perform well at one level, the organization is inclined to advance us to the next. Let me illustrate from my own illustrious career as a teenager. My first job was to pick apricots in a large orchard in Cupertino, California. I would carry two metal pails to the trees, fill them up with apricots, and then bring them back to the foreman, who would pour the apricots into wood crates. Two full pails would fill a one-bushel crate. I was confined to task work in this job and never graduated to process work.

In high school, I found a summer job on a grounds crew. We spent each day manicuring the grounds of homes and businesses. As soon as I learned the tasks, my boss elevated me to process-level accountability.

We would mow, trim, and edge the grass, weed and turn up the flower beds. He delegated more responsibility as we demonstrated the skill and willingness to perform the work at the process level. Eventually, we graduated to outcome level accountability when he felt confident that he could drop us off at a property and say, "Make it look great. I'll be back to pick you up in two hours."

As we move to outcome accountability, how we get our work done, how we accomplish our tasks, and how we manage projects and processes doesn't matter so much. It's about the outcome. When I enrolled in graduate school, the new doctoral students were invited to a meeting the first week. I can still remember listening to the vice chancellor hold forth about the mysteries of this ancient institution. I can't remember anything he said except one thing that is forever emblazoned in my memory. After his long speech, he said, "Please understand that only one in three of you will successfully complete the doctorate. The rest of you will either quit or fail. Welcome to Oxford University!"

At that moment, I seriously considered taking a bus to Heathrow and getting on a plane back to the States. Fortunately, I did stay and learned that he had not exaggerated. I also learned that the Oxford model of accountability was a pure outcome model. They granted guided autonomy with the expectation that you would make an original contribution to knowledge in your field. They were very serious about this, and my academic adviser was the embodiment of this model. He was quite willing to help me but would agree to meet only if I had something to show him. There was guidance, but no handholding, no coddling, and most importantly, no shortcuts.

Key concept: The exchange of guided autonomy for results is the basis of human performance.

This has been the consistent expectation of my professional life. When I became a manager of a consulting company based in San Francisco, my boss was in Boston, and I saw him four times a year. He seldom asked me "how" questions, but always asked me "what" and "why" questions. Every quarter he would ask, "What is your vision? What is your strategy? What are your goals and why?" If my answers were acceptable, he would say, "Great, see you next quarter." If I had a problem, he would do a deeper dive with me, but he was paying me for outcomes, and I understood that. As you can see, contributor safety is built on trust, which is a predictive understanding about the way a person will behave. My boss gave me autonomy if I delivered results.

> **Key question:** What outcomes are you expected to deliver based on the exchange of guided autonomy for results?

Blue Zone and Red Zone

Every person possesses five uniquely human characteristics:

- **Motivation: Your desire to act.** Motivation is the fuel to get up and go.
- **Volition: Your power to choose and act for yourself.** For example, right now you can choose to continue reading. Please keep reading.
- **Cognition: The mental process of learning** and the capacity of moral and rational thought. How do we do this? Through our thoughts and the five senses.
- **Emotion: Your state of feeling.** For example, you can feel joy, love, fear, surprise, or anger, which can be caused by your own thoughts and the circumstances you're in.
- **Apprehension: The state of being conscious or aware of yourself**, your thoughts and feelings, and the world around you. It's one thing to be aware, but humans also have the ability to be aware of their own awareness.

Given these defining characteristics, we realize that everyone has charge of their attention, activity, and exertions. It's a matter of personal discretion to contribute or slack off. You have discretionary effort, which is the portion of effort you choose to give beyond simple compliance. It's up to you. When a person restricts contributor safety in a way that causes us to freeze our discretionary efforts due to fear and the potential of social and emotional harm, we call that a red zone. Conversely, when a person grants contributor safety in a way that tends to release discretionary effort, we call that a blue zone (table 6).

One summer when I was a college student, I accepted my friend Joe Huston's invitation to work on a table-grape ranch in the San Joaquin Valley in California. I didn't realize that I was entering a blue zone. We worked ten hours a day in the hot sun outside the small town of Arvin, under the supervision of Joe's father, Boom Huston, the general manager of El Rancho Farms, a big operation that included packing and cold storage. The college kids worked alongside the migrant workers in an integrated crew. There were no arbitrary distinctions among us. We worked the same jobs, had the same hours, and earned the same pay. The only real difference was lunch. Their carne asada, tortillas, and salsa were better than anything I pulled out of my brown bag.

At first, I thought it was simply a matter of professional obligation that Boom treated all of us with equal respect, but it went beyond that.

Table 6 **Blue Zone/Red Zone Descriptors**

Blue Zone	Red Zone
Collaboration	Competition
Alignment	Fractures
Engagement	Silence
Confidence	Fearfulness
Risk taking	Risk aversion
Fast feedback	Slow and filtered feedback
Renewal and resilience	Burnout
Manageable stress	Debilitating stress
Self-efficacy	Self-sabotage
Initiative and resourcefulness	Learned helplessness
Creativity	Compliance

He hosted a barbecue for the workers at his home and all were invited, again without arbitrary distinctions of any kind.[2] There was no preferential treatment, just equal regard. The result of the egalitarian ethos that Boom created was highly engaged workers who were willing to release their full discretionary efforts.

> **Key question:** Do you respect only high achievers and the highly educated, or do you recognize that insight and answers can come from some of the most unlikely people?

I never saw people work so hard and smile so much. The work environment Boom created affirmed their coequal status with the other workers regardless of socioeconomic background. It offered patient encouragement for them to learn the skills to do a job without fear of a belittling response. And finally, it granted autonomy for results. Boom exacted high standards and ran a clean and organized operation, but he didn't needlessly micromanage. The contributor safety he created fueled our performance. The college kids lost their attitude and the migrant workers had a very real sense that they were not second-class citizens. Our working relationship was on equal footing.[3]

Now you might say to yourself at this point, "That's nice. Everyone worked hard and performed well because Boom made them feel good about themselves." If that were the takeaway, you would have missed the other half of the equation. Boom elevated performance in terms of raw output, but he did more than that. He planted a postindustrial mindset into a preindustrial agricultural setting. Boom was the son of the dust bowl, with parents who never finished the eighth grade, migrated to California in a Model A, and settled in Salinas. Having grown up as a cantaloupe laborer and joining the United Packinghouse Workers union at age thirteen, Boom created a blue zone from a deeply internalized sense of justice and equity.

The blue zone he created rooted out fear, allowing people to give and receive constructive feedback, collaborate by thinking out loud rather than competing in silence.[4] It emboldened people to speak up, ask for clarification, even talk about mistakes.[5] You see, it only takes a little fear to create a fear-stricken team.

> **Key concept:** Fear-stricken teams give you their hands, some of their head, and none of their heart.

They become dutiful yes men and women. The past that lingers so powerfully in the present that the "despotism of custom" hinders human achievement, as John Stuart Mill observed during England's Industrial Revolution. If I'm overstating the case, why, then, does Gallup continue to report that 85 percent of employees worldwide are "not engaged or actively disengaged at work," resulting in a global downward trend in workplace productivity?[6] Why do we constantly launch anti-harassment campaigns in our corporations? We have some work to do.

> **Key question:** Do you express any nonverbal cues that might silently marginalize others and create a red zone?

I walked away from my experience in California's Central Valley with the very real conviction that most people will release their discretionary efforts if they are working in a climate of contributor safety. If given the chance, they will produce outstanding results in exchange for autonomy, guidance, and support.

> **Key questions:** When have you worked in a blue zone? When have you worked in a red zone? How would you describe your motivation in each case?

Every person regulates his or her own discretionary effort, and the internal regulator we use is very sensitive to the way others treat us. On one occasion, I took my son to the doctor. This doctor was a well-respected specialist. He came into the room, didn't make eye contact with us, didn't say hello, didn't even raise his eyes above his clipboard. "OK, what seems to be the problem?" he asked. He quickly examined my son and wrote a prescription. And then he was gone. As we walked out of the office, my son turned to me and said, "Dad, he's a terrible doctor and I don't ever want to come back." Turns out his diagnosis and treatment were correct. He was a competent physician. But that's not the whole job, is it? What was my son observing? He was observing human interaction. Why did he have such an allergic reaction to this doctor? His skills were first-rate, but his demeanor was either aloof or indifferent.

In case you're tempted to dismiss my last example as simply a matter of an introverted personality, which we sometimes use as an excuse for ourselves, consider two presidents of the United States—George Washington and Abraham Lincoln. They were by anyone's estimation incredible leaders who changed the history of the world. But if we take a closer look, we realize that they were miles apart in basic temperament and disposition. Washington had a commanding presence and yet was an awkward speaker. Lincoln, on the other hand, had an awkward presence and was a commanding speaker. Washington was stately, dignified, formal, detached, quiet, and reserved. Lincoln was informal and personable and would lighten the mood with jokes, humor, and storytelling. And yet despite their big differences in personality, they nurtured contributor safety. They both had the ability to recruit the best people and enlist their highest service even when those very people were filled with envy and resentment toward them.

Let me repeat the point: Don't excuse yourself from the obligation of creating contributor safety because you think you may not possess certain gifts of personality. I had an English teacher in high school, Mr. Westergard, who I thought was a rather austere man. He never said much, and yet I could sense that he respected me. My advice would be to avoid extremes. If you're Spock-like in demeanor, people won't know you care. If you're effusive, the emotional display can be tiresome. In any situation, we must exercise emotional intelligence by governing our interactions with composure. In the fourth century BC, Aristotle tutored us about the need for this poise and moderation. "Emotions may be felt both too much and too little, and in both cases not well;

but to feel them at the right times, with reference to the right objects, towards the right people, with the right motive, and in the right way."[7] Be yourself. Just be your best self.

> **Key question:** Do you have a clear sense of how your demeanor and behavior are perceived by others? Even if you think you do, ask five people who know you well to answer that question.

Are You Emotionally Prepared to Create Contributor Safety?

On one occasion, I made what I call a charisma hire: I confused rhetorical talent and showmanship for leadership. I paid the price. Here's how it went down: I had to let a sales manager go and was looking for a replacement. In walked a very experienced, polished, and highly impressive candidate. She was a superstar with the education, drive, and track record—everything that would normally indicate certain success. On top of it all, she had charisma—that ineffable quality that can be so dangerous because it is more stylistic than substantive. It can blind even experienced leaders from asking tough questions about a person's background, experience, and qualifications, turning due diligence into negligence. On this occasion, I became willfully blind. This individual had such a commanding presence and was so utterly convincing in her claim that she could double sales in two years, that I got sucked in and spent the next eighteen months regretting it.

The month after I promoted her, I returned to the office where she worked with her team. The office registered a subzero temperature. My employees were silent, moved in slow motion, and wore painted smiles. What on earth had happened in the space of thirty days? I started pulling people aside to find out. As one of the employees put it, "The reign of terror has begun." Regrettably, while this new executive was incredibly talented, she was not emotionally prepared to create contributor safety. The reality is that whether you're in a leadership role or an individual contributor role, you have the responsibility to help create contributor safety for the team. Ask yourself if you are emotionally prepared to do it.

Key question: Can you be genuinely happy for the success of others?

The question you should ask yourself is why anyone would want to be led by you? You can always lay down the law and point out that it's part of the social contract of being a member of this family or this team or this pit crew or this SWOT team or this stage crew. If you pull that card, you're resorting to compliance and confessing your inability to motivate and summon discretionary effort. What about commitment? How do you get people to want to perform? We've been asking that question for millennia and we know at least one thing: people need contributor safety.

I've seen many cases in which a frightening and cruel environment extracted a great deal of labor from people. Yes, but what kind? Mindless labor, resentful labor, low-productivity labor. And for how long? I've never seen a toxic work environment produce high performance and sustain it over time. A toxic environment is one in which employees are motivated by personal gain to the point that they engage in mean-spirited comments, unethical behavior, abuse, and bullying.

Key concept: A toxic environment shuts down performance because people worry about psychological safety before they worry about performance.

If we are prudently managing risk, and the individual is capable and doing his or her part, we should grant as much autonomy as we can. But sometimes we don't. Why would someone withhold contributor safety?

Key question: Have you ever withheld contributor safety from someone when they had earned it?

Remember, contributor safety is an earned privilege. Despite an individual's readiness to contribute his or her skill, competence, and experience, we often deny it for illegitimate reasons, including the arrogance or insecurity of the leader, personal or institutional bias, prejudice or discrimination, prevailing team norms that reinforce insensitivity, a lack of empathy, or aloofness. Contributor safety results when the individual can contribute, and the leader and team members are able to manage their egos.

Increase Your Powers of Observation

To foster the high level of contributor safety needed for a blue zone, you must get to know the members of your team. That means spending time with them, studying their individual dispositions, and then listening intently to what they say. In fact, if you listen long enough, people will often reveal what they would otherwise conceal.

Finally, watch them in action and pay attention to the way they contribute. Some of your people are natural collaborators. They thrive on dialogue. They relish problem-solving as a social process. They love banter and the repartee of hard-hitting give-and-take. But others can't stand it. They love problem-solving as an internal process. They love to deconstruct problems and think through solutions but wouldn't think of fighting for airtime in a discussion. They may be more reflective and solitary, and yet they possess first-rate critical thinking skills.

If you as the leader don't develop higher powers of observation, if you don't watch the way everyone responds to social cues, if you think leadership is a performance and you're the show, your tone deafness could deal a fatal blow to your team. Here's a way to run a quick diagnostic to check yourself.

Key concept: Leaders spend most of their time engaged in inquiry and advocacy.

You're either trying to figure something out or you're trying to convince others that you have it figured out. This is largely what leaders do. Obviously, these two things translate into two clear behavioral patterns. When you're engaged in inquiry, when you're trying to figure something out, when you're in discovery mode, what are you doing as you participate in dialogue or discussion? That's right, you're asking questions. On the other hand, if you're engaged in advocacy, trying to influence others toward your point of view, what are you doing? Right again, you're telling. Figure 9 shows the tell-to-ask continuum.

The Tell-to-Ask Continuum

What's your tell-to-ask ratio? Track yourself for a day or so and figure out how much of the time you're telling versus asking. I've sat in way too many meetings in which the boss is telling everyone what to do and everyone nods politely. Telling is efficient, but it quickly moves the listener into a passive mode and can slow down learning. The entire culture of major college football is steeped in an industrial model of tell. Just watch coach-to-player interactions: The coach is talking, talking, talking, and the players stand there and nod their heads at the end of each exchange. No wonder it takes so long to develop football IQ.

Over a period of four years, I spent endless hours in practice and team meetings, listening to coaches and watching film. Was it collaborative? Was it true dialogue? Was it active intellectual engagement? Not remotely. The signal-to-noise ratio (the amount of signal compared to the amount of background noise) gets so low that as a player you simply stop listening. The coach's incessant telling voice eventually becomes part of the noise. Here's how it would go:

"Clark, look at your body angle. You came off the line too slow. I don't know why your hand placement is that way. You've got to get lower and stop your man's momentum. Read the linemen's stance. Look at how much weight they put on their hands. That will tell you if it's a run play. Look at the tackle's first step. What's he doing? He's trying

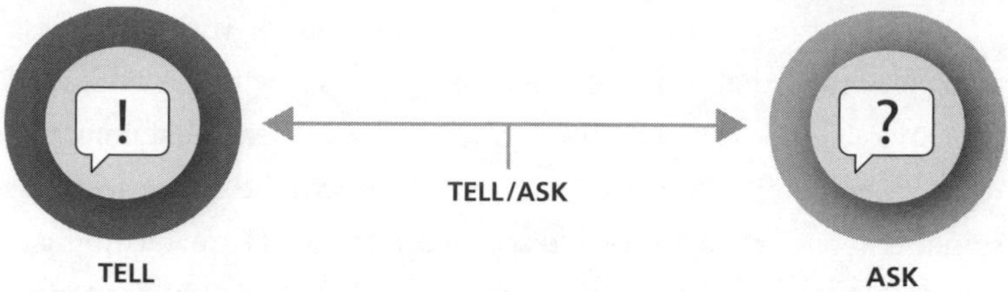

Figure 9. Telling and asking: opposite behaviors of a leader

to draw you inside. You know they run this draw-trap play almost every series." And it goes on and on. Can you imagine how our progress would have accelerated if my coaches had shifted from tell to ask, if they had handed me the remote control and said, "Clark, here's the next play. Please take us through it. Break it down"? It would have transformed culture and performance.

> **Key concept:** A leader's tell-to-ask ratio shapes the signal-to-noise ratio for the team. If the leader is telling all the time, that telling becomes noise.

Can you see the risk? Some of the most wonderful, kind-hearted people I know are stuck at the tell end of the coaching continuum, and that is the root of their problem. They lead teams of talented people but are unable to draw them out because they are in chronic and perpetual advocacy mode, which lowers the signal-to-noise ratio. Their voices become noise to their listeners. As I said, some team members are willing to take this on and jump into the fray, and it's all good fun to them. But the quiet, contemplative, introverted, and often brilliant ones take a pass because it's not their natural habitat.

> **Key question:** What's your tell-to-ask ratio?

Listen Carefully, Speak Last

I once worked with a group of high-potential leaders at a technology company in Silicon Valley. They had been nominated to participate in a six-month leadership program to accelerate their development and prepare them for further responsibility. The team I worked with had to work virtually with each other because it consisted of members from nearly every continent. As a capstone to their cohort experience, they were given the assignment to make a major strategic recommendation to the company's executive team. The long-awaited day finally came for the team to make their pitch. The members of the team flew in from their respective office locations a day early to rehearse their presentation. They had worked weekends and made tremendous personal sacrifices to get to this point, and now they were ready to make their pitch.

They used every second of the allocated thirty minutes to make a well-researched and beautifully choreographed presentation. The agenda called for thirty minutes of Q&A to follow. Visibly exhausted and yet satisfied with their performance, they turned eagerly to the executive team for feedback. To everyone's amazement, the CEO spoke first. In a monotone voice and no visual display of emotion, he matter-of-factly said he thought the proposal was good but would cost too much money to pursue. He droned on for ten minutes about the company's strategy and priorities. Can you guess what happened next? That's right. Nothing. The other executives didn't make a peep. The meeting disbanded after the CEO's sermonic performance and the crestfallen team moved to a neighboring conference room, where I spent the next hour helping them de-escalate their anger and frustration.

The next week I debriefed with several of the executives and asked that they let the CEO know that the next time it would be better for him to speak last, after the other executives had asked their questions and expressed their views.

> **Key concept:** Speaking first when you hold positional power softly censors your team.

Not long after, I heard back that the feedback had indeed been delivered to the CEO. Well, the story doesn't end there. We ran the same program the following year. The new team was given the same assignment. They made a similar investment of time and effort and arrived at the appointed day to make their presentation. Following a similarly well-vetted and well-crafted presentation, the CEO did the very same thing. He shut them down in the first five minutes of Q&A. He wasn't rude or mean in what he said or the way he said it. But by virtue of his position he brought the process to a swift and ignominious end. He was obtuse, insensitive, and self-indulgent.

Key question: Are you emotionally advanced beyond needing to hear yourself talk?

Help Others Think beyond Their Roles

One of the most powerful things you can do to engender contributor safety is help the members of your team think beyond their individual roles. Surely, you've seen how the boundaries of a person's role tend to confine thinking to the role. We become small and siloed in our perspectives instead of getting up in our hot-air balloon to see the whole and how the parts fit together.

When people join an organization, they normally join a team that is part of a function or department. And the first thing they do is learn to perform basic tasks that relate to their specific role. If I'm in marketing, I may learn how to launch a Google ad word campaign; if I'm in accounting, I may learn how to reconcile the inventory; if I'm in purchasing, I may learn how to review a new potential vendor; if I'm in engineering, I may learn how to write code to make our application more mobile compatible; if I'm in sales, I may learn how to give a product demo. You get the picture. The point is that most of us grow up in organizations with a task-based, tactical mindset. We perform our roles and we get good at what we do.

But increasingly, especially in highly dynamic environments, the team needs us to contribute in our roles *and* think beyond our roles.

What does this require? It requires that we have both the skill and the will to make that bigger contribution. Here's how the skill side of it normally plays out: One day the organization taps you on the shoulder and says, "Hey, I need you to think strategically. Go and be strategic!" And you say, "That sounds great. How do I do that?"

"I'm not sure, but go do it," comes the reply.

Sound familiar? This scenario repeats itself over and over in organizations. So let's back up. To think beyond your role, you need both skill and will. I should have said will and skill. The sequence matters. Do you find people attempting to think and contribute beyond their roles if they don't feel confident and safe to at least try?

> **Key concept:** Before people can get out of their tactical and functional siloes to think strategically, they must be liberated by the contributor safety you give them.

I once worked with a gentleman who was the vice president of procurement for a Fortune 500 organization. He lorded over his people as if he were the hereditary monarch and they were peasants. In one meeting, he chided his people for not thinking more strategically about the company's overall purchasing strategy and the need to squeeze the list of approved suppliers. In effect, he was asking them to think and contribute beyond their roles without supplying support. He had some people with incredible potential. I came back a year later and he still had some people with incredible potential.

Helping others think beyond their roles starts with an opportunity and a direct invitation. In our company, we invite the software development team to think about our marketing strategy. We invite sales to think about software development. It's not something we spend time on every day, but we deliberately ask each employee to think beyond his or her role.

> **Key principle:** The invitation to think beyond one's role expresses greater respect for the individual and grants greater permission to contribute.

The way you do it makes all the difference. You still need people to stay focused on their primary roles. I've seen some leaders get carried away with an unbounded sense of collaboration that resulted in chaos. Be deliberate about the topics or challenges you want to address and make specific invitations to address those issues. Then issue a standing invitation for ideas and suggestions on any aspect of performance, with the understanding that you will always be heard but not always heeded.

Finally, to prevent a team's descent into chaos, the leader must know when constructive dissent is giving way to destructive derailment.

> **Key concept:** It's the leader's job to recognize the difference between dissenting and derailing behavior and to manage the boundary between the two.

It's one thing to disagree or to offer an alternative point of view with an attitude to contribute based on a sense of where the team is and whether the alternative is viable. It's quite another to dissent in a way that is disruptive to team morale and not helpful to overall progress. Those who dissent constructively are guided by a sense of self-awareness and pure intent. Those who dissent destructively are misguided by a personal agenda and a lack of self-awareness.

Conclusion

If you want to foster a blue zone of contributor safety, create a truly collaborative environment. If your style is heavy-handed, your communication didactic, and your ego fragile, you will scorch any seedling of contributor safety that's beginning to shoot up. Remember, you set the tone for your team's mode of execution. If you're not a leader by position and must lead by influence only, which is the case for most of us, create contributor safety in the same way.

The level of contributor safety on your team is expressed by the invitation to contribute that you extend to each person to jump into action. It's your culture on display and your DNA in action. It's how you give and take, push and pull, talk and listen, question and answer, act and react, analyze and solve. Remember, people want to play in the game!

Key Concepts

- Except for those who may be paralyzed by fear or anxiety, human beings have a deep and unrelenting drive to play in the game.
- The preparation to perform creates the desire to perform.
- Organizations engage in only two processes—execution and innovation. Execution is the creation and delivery of value today, while innovation is the creation and delivery of value tomorrow.
- Offensive innovation is a response to an opportunity, while defensive innovation is a response to a threat or crisis.
- When an external threat challenges the status quo, the natural fear of challenging the status quo is replaced with the survival instinct.
- When your competent and willing to hold yourself accountable, you're ready to receive contributor safety.
- The exchange of autonomy for results is the basis of human performance.
- Fear-stricken teams give you their hands, some of their head, and none of their heart.
- A toxic environment shuts down performance because people worry about psychological safety before they worry about performance.
- Leaders spend most of their time engaged in inquiry and advocacy.
- A leader's tell-to-ask ratio shapes the signal-to-noise ratio for the team. If the leader is telling all the time, that telling becomes noise.

- Speaking first when you hold positional power softly censors your team.
- Before people can get out of their tactical and functional siloes to think strategically, they have to be liberated by the contributor safety you give them.
- The invitation to think beyond one's role expresses greater respect for the individual and grants greater permission to contribute.
- It's the leader's job to recognize the difference between dissenting and derailing behavior and manage the boundary between the two.

Key Questions

- Have you ever had an external threat that removed the fear of challenging the status quo?
- Have you ever granted contributor safety too fast when the person either didn't have the skill or wasn't willing to assume responsibility for the results?
- What outcomes are you expected to deliver based on the exchange of autonomy for results?
- Do you respect only high achievers and the highly educated, or do you recognize that insight and answers can come from some of the most unlikely people?
- Do you express any nonverbal cues that might silently marginalize others and create a red zone?
- When have you worked in a blue zone? When have you worked in a red zone? How would you describe your motivation in each case?
- Do you have a clear sense of how your demeanor and behavior are perceived by others? Even if you think you do, ask five people who know you well to answer that question.
- Can you be genuinely happy for the success of others?

- Have you ever withheld contributor safety from someone when they had earned it?
- What's your tell-to-ask ratio?
- Are you emotionally advanced beyond needing to hear yourself talk?

STAGE 4

Challenger Safety

Every society has its protectors of status quo and its fraternities of the indifferent who are notorious for sleeping through revolutions. Today, our very survival depends on our ability to stay awake, to adjust to new ideas, to remain vigilant and to face the challenge of change.

—Martin Luther King Jr.

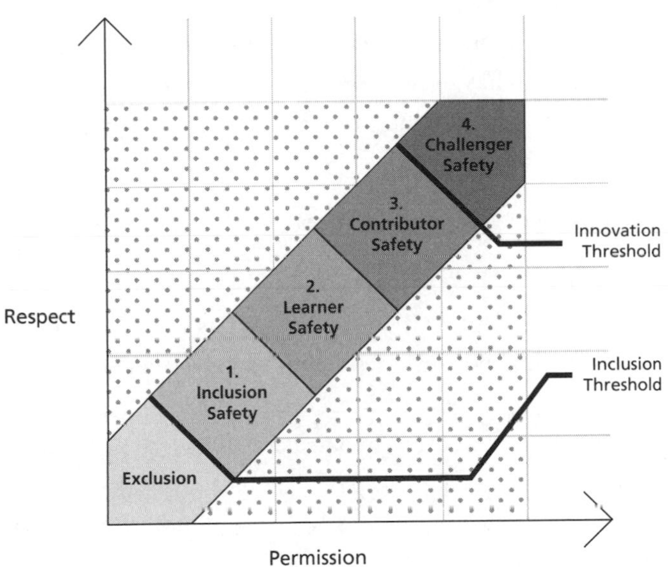

Figure 10. The last stage on the path to inclusion and innovation

The Neuroplasticity of Teams

Brain researchers used to think that the circuitry of the brain was fixed. They have since learned that the hundred billion neurons and hundred trillion connections among those neurons operate in an incredibly flexible way. The brain has plasticity and can rewire itself. A team is nothing less than a great brain. But the synapses take place between people rather than between neurons. Similarly, there is nothing fixed or hardwired about the speed or patterns of these connections. Teams are astonishingly plastic, so we really don't know the natural capacity of any team to perform. We simply know they can surprise us because the human ingenuity of a given group of people is unknown and unknowable. More than anything else, team plasticity reflects the leader's modeling behavior. If the leader suppresses dissent, people recoil as predictably as deer react to sudden movements. If the leader accommodates dissent, it builds the team's innovation-surge capacity. Collectively, the team has sensory organs that react to the environment, adapting based on social, emotional, and intellectual processing of the conditions that surround it.

Key question: What patterns has your team adopted from the leader?

I once worked with a CEO whose team was struggling to adapt in a rapidly changing industry. He said his team was not smart enough, curious enough, or entrepreneurial enough. When his amygdala overpowered his prefrontal cortex, he acted out of frustration. The tenor of the team changed. His efforts to "drive" innovation would always result in a blowback of crippling silence. As fear extinguished curiosity, the team became sluggish, stubborn, and slow.

Key concept: Challenger safety democratizes innovation.

After posting lackluster results for a couple of years, this feudal lord was fired. Fortunately, I had the pleasure of working with his successor. The anatomy of the executive team didn't change, but the environment did. The new leader introduced a new social technology—none other than challenger safety (figure 10, page 95). He nurtured respect and permission to astonishing levels. He brought down the cultural barriers to entry. The team was a little skittish at first, but then came a wave of unprecedented productivity. You see, humans are designed to respond to kindness and empathy.[1] They responded with improvement after improvement, innovation after innovation. The new CEO regenerated the neurological system of the team. The velocity of information increased. The cocreative process came alive. The adaptive capacity emerged. He took the team to intellectual heights they had never known. As a unit, they became more artistic and more athletic, more disciplined and more demanding, and ultimately, much more confident and aware of themselves.

Key concept: When it comes to innovation, connectivity increases productivity.

The changes in inputs brought changes in outputs. Here came the flow of insights, connections, associations, ideations, unexpected leaps, and aha moments. This is the promise of challenger safety. You can do the same thing this leader did if you encourage dialogue and emotionally tolerate dissent along the way. Because people are creative within a cultural context, it's the leader's job to liberate the creative impulse in that context.[2]

Now here's the other side of it: Although the brain is plastic, it defaults to rigidity. Teams do too, which means that the past lingers in the present. The early socialization patterns and original norms tend to be incredibly stubborn and hard to replace.

Key concept: To socialize a team with challenger safety from the beginning is always easier than to re-socialize a team later.

Organizational change is a process that moves through three separate layers—technical, behavioral, and cultural. We often start by changing all three layers at the same time, but each one changes at a different pace. First is the structural or nonhuman layer, or what we call artifacts. They include systems, processes, structures, roles, responsibilities, policies, procedures, and tools and technology. These things represent configurable parts and can be changed relatively quickly with money and authority. In the behavioral layer, we change the way people behave as they interact with the technical layer and each other in new ways. But simply because people are behaving differently doesn't mean that they want to or that they would continue in the new patterns if given the choice. When artifacts hold up behavior, they act as scaffolding, and once the scaffolding is removed, behavior reverts to past patterns—unless there are changes in the cultural layer. That tendency to snap back is what we call a regression to the mean. The third layer of change is the invisible layer, consisting of values, beliefs, and assumptions.

Key question: Can you think of a change you started but didn't finish, where you snapped back to your original behavior?

In all social units, the cultural layer is the single most difficult thing to change and the layer that changes last. It's your lag indicator. You can impose change and get people to comply. If the chief medical officer at a hospital is watching, the doctors and nurses will wash their hands to decrease the risk of nosocomial infection. But if the chief steps away, their level of compliance immediately falls. Why? Because they lack intrinsic motivation. They go back to their calcified patterns.

Team behavior is much the same. What compounds the problem in challenger safety is that you are asking people not only to change their behavior but to do it in an environment of greater personal risk.

The Stage of Brave

The culminating stage of psychological safety is the place where respect and permission intersect at the highest level—a super-enriched zone dedicated to exploration and experimentation. To advance from contributor safety to challenger safety requires crossing the "innovation threshold"—a place where the highest possible level of psychological safety replaces what would normally be a place inhabited with the greatest fear. But creating challenger safety is far more difficult than understanding it. It's the ultimate cultural quest for every leader.

Challenger safety is a level of psychological safety so high that people feel empowered to challenge the status quo, leaving their comfort zones to put a creative or disruptive idea on the table, which by definition, is a threat to the way things are done and therefore a risk to themselves personally. To invite people to challenge the status quo is both natural and unnatural. It's natural in the sense that human beings are innately creative. The biologist Edward O. Wilson said creativity is "the unique and defining trait of our species."[3] The creative instinct propels us to challenge the status quo out of a desire to create and improve things, but doing so is unnatural in an environment that we perceive to be unsafe. If the environment is a pocket of thick trust, we will go forward with our challenge. If it's a pocket of thin trust, our self-censoring instinct is triggered, and we will remove ourselves from participation. The atmosphere either draws out or shuts down the creative impulse to challenge. It's scary enough to speak truth to power. It's even more scary to speak opinion to power because there's a bigger personal risk of rejection and embarrassment.

I recently interviewed a vice president at a large health care system. He said the organization was more militaristic than the military. He challenged the status quo on a staffing issue early on and barely lived to tell about it. "I thought I had a brain, but I guess I don't," he said. "In this organization, you do exactly what you're told, with no commentary." I interviewed another woman who worked at a large media company in South America. "We are not allowed to be creative," she said. "If you're not in senior leadership, you don't challenge anything. If you do, you're out."

Clearly, not all leaders are convinced that psychological safety is necessary for innovation. As a result, some leaders believe that psychological safety is nothing more than asking people to be nice, under the assumption that they need to be coddled before they can be expected to engage. Two Australian scholars, Ben Farr-Wharton and Ace Simpson, make this point masterfully. "Through a systems management perspective, the very human concept of compassion seems wasteful. This is because noticing, empathizing with, making sense of and responding to a colleague's suffering (how we define the process of organizational compassion) may be considered an indulgent and time-consuming process that detracts from immediate work duties."[4]

Those who say that psychological safety is nothing more than sympathetic and sentimental slush offered by leaders who are unwilling to hold others accountable are in denial themselves. They refuse to acknowledge that you can't coerce or manipulate innovation. The process is surrounded by political and interpersonal risk. Unless you lower or remove those barriers to entry and those violations in human interaction, people simply will not engage at full capacity.

This final stage of psychological safety governs what are clearly the most sensitive, charged, pressurized, politicized, stressful, and high-stakes situations of all. Because the fear and potential risk to the individual are highest, the level of psychological safety must be deepest. With inclusion safety, you're asking to be included; with learner safety, you're asking to be encouraged; with contributor safety, you're asking for autonomy; but with challenger safety, the social exchange has now gone to another level: The team is asking you to challenge the status quo. That's a mighty ask! Thus, the only reasonable condition is that the organization protect you in the process. If the organization wants candor, you need cover—you need real and sustained air cover to be brave enough to take what is almost always a substantial personal risk.

In case it still hasn't sunk in, let me sketch the emotional landscape of innovation in an organization. It's one thing to use your talents in creative pursuits or be curious about something on your own. It's quite another to take aim at the status quo in an organization when the entire system and culture preserve it. If challenger safety doesn't exist in the organization, there's a high cost to that curiosity and creativity. It tends to be an arena of shame, pain, and embarrassment in addition to the normal uncertainty, ambiguity, and chaos. Innovation is hard enough because there's no safety from failure. No one can give you that. But what the leader can do is take the social sting and emotional bite out of the process. At a minimum, the absence of challenger safety blocks the flow of information that allows collaboration to happen.

For organizations trying to create a thriving environment for neurodivergent talent, including employees who demonstrate variations in learning, attention, mood, and sociability—including the autism spectrum, dyslexia, attention deficit, hyperactivity, depression, and other atypical neurological conditions—challenger safety becomes a precondition for basic productivity. It's my personal experience that neurodivergent employees are more acutely sensitive to indicators of fear, react faster to them, and require more time to reemerge out of defensive routines. And yet we all need challenger safety to help us be brave enough to challenge the status quo.

> **Key question:** When was the last time you were brave and challenged the status quo?

When I teach leaders the concept of challenger safety and the social exchange of candor for cover, they often nod and say, "I got it." That's when I stare back at them and say, "No, you don't got that. You don't even begin to get the magnitude of what you are asking people to do." May I suggest at this point that you put this book down and go find a mirror. Now take a hard look. If you want your people to innovate, you need to do some soul-searching and deep introspection about what you're asking. Innovation is not some kind of frictionless, comfortable process. No, innovation is doing violence to the current regime. It's willfully knocking yourself out of orbit. It's trading certainty for ambiguity. Most of the time, it's asking for failure. That's just the organizational side of it. Now think about the personal side.

What are you asking of your people when you ask them to challenge the status quo and innovate? Yes, there's a sense of adventure that comes with exploration, but the reality is that you're asking your people to expose themselves to criticism, risk failure, take chances, be vulnerable, not fit in, and feel pain. And you're asking them to do all of this without any real control of the outcome.

Now do you see what you're asking? Well, if you're going to ask that, your employees are going to make a reasonable request of you. They know you can't promise zero loss. They know you can't remove all risk, and they know you can't eliminate the pain. Everybody gets that, so at a minimum, they're asking you to protect them socially and emotionally as they engage in this free-ranging process. "At least protect me from embarrassment and rejection" comes the petition. Now that's a reasonable request. And don't forget that not everyone craves creative contribution over comfort.

Which brings us to the question of who goes first. I was training a group of employees at a university once and sat down at one of the tables to join a discussion. One of the participants said, "I get the candor-for-cover concept. Would you please tell the executives that the cover must come first? Do they really expect me to give the candor when I haven't seen evidence of the cover? I may be dumb, but I'm not stupid." There you have it.

Candor for cover means that you as the leader protect each person's right to speak candidly about any topic, provided they don't make personal attacks or have malicious intent. When people feel protected in that right, they tend to exercise that right (see table 7).

Key concept: The social exchange for challenger safety is cover for candor.

The definition of *respect* in the fourth stage of psychological safety is "respect for the individual's ability to innovate." Like the definitions of respect for learner safety and contributor safety, respect at this level is an earned right rather than an innate right. Thus, you earn the right

Table 7 **Stage 4 Challenger Safety**

Stage	Definition of Respect	Definition of Permission	Social Exchange
1. Inclusion safety	Respect for the individual's humanity	Permission for the individual to interact with you as a human being	Inclusion in exchange for human status and the absence of harm
2. Learner safety	Respect for the individual's innate need to learn and grow	Permission for the individual to engage in all aspects of the learning process	Encouragement in exchange for engagement
3. Contributor safety	Respect for the individual's ability to create value	Permission for the individual to work with independence and their own judgment	Autonomy with guidance in exchange for results
4. Challenger safety	Respect for the individual's ability to innovate	Permission for the individual to challenge the status quo in good faith	Cover in exchange for candor

to innovate based on a track record of performance. Am I saying you shouldn't have a voice until you become an expert? No, everyone should have a voice, but you will naturally find that people will take you seriously if that voice has credibility behind it.

In addition to respect, the nature of permission changes as well as we transition to challenger safety. In the fourth stage, implicitly or explicitly, we are giving the individual permission to challenge the status quo in good faith. That means we assume the individual is acting with pure motive to help improve things. There are no other qualifications or restrictions. Sometimes people challenge the status quo with ideas for incremental improvement. Sometimes they take moon shots and propose a wholesale transformation to the way we do things. Sometimes they come with fully baked ideas and plans, and sometimes they come with nothing but an unsupported hunch or gut instinct. In an atmosphere of challenger safety, we take all comers and all contributions. We may take some challenges more seriously than others as we consider the source, but we honor each person's offering regardless of hierarchy. We make it safe to criticize. Everyone is expected to engage in disruptive thinking.

> **Key question:** Do you feel that you have a license to innovate in your organization?

If you have challenged the status quo without challenger safety, you no doubt remember that painful experience, and you're very careful not to repeat it. Your brave attempt was met with retribution. You thought you had the air cover, but you were wrong, which left you naked to rejection. Those experiences are neurobiological encounters that create stress, scars, and vivid memories that cause us to err on the side of caution the next time.

On one occasion, I was training a large law enforcement agency. I sensed right away that the culture was toxic and vindictive. Sure enough, as soon as we moved into the first discussion, you could plainly see that the members of this organization were not healthy enough to hold even a basic dialogue. By imposing the constant fear of criticism, the leaders had successfully created an atmosphere of jaded cynicism. The group dynamic was silence interspersed with sarcasm, an occasional wisecrack, and cutting humor. No one would dare challenge the status quo in good faith. That would be tantamount to a request for verbal and emotional abuse, which would come swiftly.

If you're encouraging your people to challenge the status quo but haven't prepared the climate by cultivating the necessary challenger safety, what can you reasonably expect? Are your people going to be brave and wander into enemy territory when they know their bravery will be met with punishment? Do people volunteer opinions when opinions are suppressed?[5] Only fools rush in when it's not safe. If there's no air cover to back them up, it's unwise of them to try and disingenuous of you to ask. Even if you frame challenging the status quo as expressing healthy dissatisfaction, it's still subversive and always a personal risk. No cover, no candor. People will come up with defensive routines to save themselves from the risk of embarrassment.[6] And if they make mistakes, they will be sorely tempted to cover them up.

> **Key questions:** When was the last time you tried to cover up a mistake? What motivated you to do that?

Let me illustrate from my own professional experience. For three years I had a Japanese boss based in Tokyo, Mr. Tadao Otsuki. When I was given the assignment to report to him, I braced myself because of what I had read about the rigid hierarchical nature of Japanese business culture. I read a book about Japanese society that issued this warning: "An expression of a contradictory opinion to that of the head was considered a sign of misbehavior."[7] "I'm in trouble," I thought, because I don't know how to do my job without giving my opinions, and sometimes they are bound to be contrary. But then came the pleasant surprise: Tad turned out to be a collaborative, trustworthy man who allowed me to be brave. He cultivated an idea meritocracy and was utterly agnostic about title, position, and authority, leveling the power dynamics and draining the anxiety out of the process of seeking help or feedback, and feeling vulnerable when you did.[8] In the twilight of his career, this man had worked for several multinational corporations and had learned that diverse, multidisciplinary teams don't innovate unless they are lubricated with the oil of challenger safety. He understood that innovation requires exploring the unknown and always involves tension and stress. He asked me to be brave, but first created the organization's accommodation for that bravery, which of course would mean that I would often offer up bad ideas or go down dead-end roads. But then there were times when the team would come up with breakthrough innovations.

Key question: Do you strive to be agnostic about title, position, or authority when someone challenges the status quo?

As a last step to set the table for challenger safety, he demonstrated transparency. He shared all the information he could, and he did it consistently.

Key concept: The more unknowns the leader eliminates through transparency, the fewer sources of stress the employee worries about.

I accepted the invitation. I ventured out slowly, observing my boss carefully for any signs of emotional defensiveness. Eventually, I quit fearing failure or judgment because it was, as Abraham Maslow put it, "safe enough to dare."[9] It was never a career ender to challenge something because I knew the culture tolerated and even expected it. It's the leader that creates that organizational laboratory of experimentation, and that lab requires conditions that are different from a pure execution mode of operations. Think about the inherent constraints under which we must innovate. Typically, we have less data, more ambiguity, more unknowns, and more failures, so we need more exploratory inquiry, more tolerance for unreasonable ideas, and more capacity to absorb failure.[10]

Clearly, innovation most often happens under conditions of stress, when you're feeling the pressure of competition, when you're trying to figure out a solution surrounded by constraints and limitations. There's nothing relaxed or carefree about it.

Key concept: In the process of innovation, there is no necessary relationship between stress and fear.

The stress and pressure we feel doesn't automatically create fear. I remember many times working for Tad when I felt enormous pressure and exhilaration. The pressure was imposed by our competitive circumstances, but he didn't add a layer of fear to the mix as a perverse incentive to get us motivated. By creating challenger safety, he helped convert stress into positive energy. I had been put in charge of an organization that was hemorrhaging cash. The market tanked and we were in a free fall. Instead of escalating interpersonal tension to accompany the crisis, my boss increased the frequency of his touch points with me, but they were always calm and focused encounters. Even when others showed up with spiked emotion, Tad was a de-escalating influence. Eventually, we came through the crisis with a stronger, faster, and more engaged organization.

Key concept: It's possible to unlock creativity in a crisis if the leader welcomes dissent and doesn't add a layer of manufactured fear to the existing level of natural stress.

The Social Origins of Innovation

Innovation means looking into the foggy future and trying to make something better by connecting things that are not normally connected using divergent, lateral, associative, or nonlinear thinking. You basically have three options. You can connect

- Existing knowledge with existing knowledge
- Existing knowledge with new knowledge
- New knowledge with new knowledge

Remember a few years ago when Netflix knocked Blockbuster out of the market? How did they do it? They connected snail mail with compact discs! Those two ordinary things became the source of an unlikely, disruptive innovation. That's the pattern most of the time. We build on what we know, using the tools, technology, and ideas we already have.[11] How do you think chocolate and peanut butter came together? But here's the irony of innovation: even though it's built on knowledge assets, it's the learning process that brings them together to create value in new ways.

Key concept: In the process of innovation, learning is more important than knowing.

Learning is the process of combining knowledge assets, but those assets are constantly becoming obsolete. In the long run, an enduring and adaptable learning process is more valuable than the perishable knowledge assets themselves.

If we look at innovation further, we can see that there are two basic types. Type 1 is incremental and derivative, while type 2 is radical and disruptive (table 8).

Table 8 **The Two Types of Innovation**

TYPE 1	TYPE 2
• Incremental • Derivative	• Radical • Disruptive

Key question: Can you think of a recent example of type 1 innovation (incremental and derivative) in your organization?

As you might expect, type 1 is much more common because it's natural to start with what we know and connect it with something else that we know. If that doesn't work, we try new combinations of things (figure 11). We combine and recombine. That recombination is the essence of innovation. That's why Steve Jobs said, "Creativity is just connecting things." I'd like to add to that statement.

Key concept: Innovation is the process of connected people connecting things.

We all know that simply putting a bunch of virtuosos together doesn't automatically create beautiful music. They must learn to play together. They must connect first, and out of that connection comes the magic.

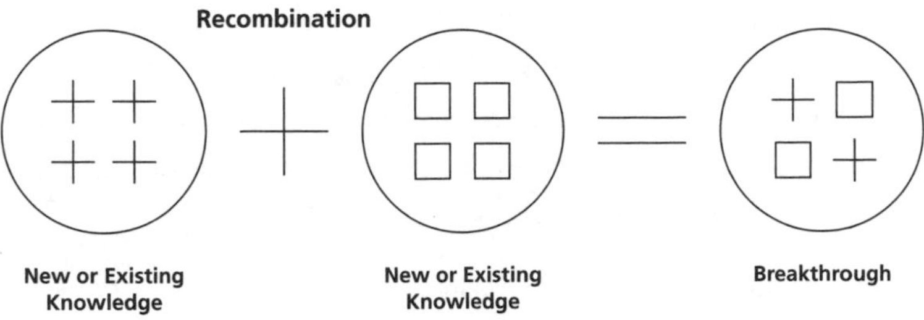

Figure 11. How breakthroughs are generated

The Process of Innovation

People can of course experience a light bulb moment of lone genius, a burst of inspiration, a eureka moment, but those are the exception. The more common pattern is for innovation to spring out of social interaction. In a Q&A session at Facebook, Mark Zuckerberg said, "Ideas typically do not just come to you. They happen because you've been talking about something and talking to a lot of people about it for a long period of time."[12] Brian Wilson, the musical genius behind the Beach Boys, confessed the same truth: "The key to our success was respecting one another's ideas and opinions."[13] Yes, you need talented people to innovate, but the magic is in the way they blend and merge ideas as they work together in what often seems a chaotic and spontaneous process. It doesn't matter if you are writing software or writing music, innovation usually has a social origin.

Are Questions Welcome?

I invite you to be a cultural anthropologist for a day and watch the way innovation happens on your team. If you look carefully, you'll notice that innovation ultimately emerges from the process of inquiry. That process comprises five steps, as shown in figure 12.

As you can see, the first step is to ask questions. Questions act as the catalyst. They activate the process. Without questions, nothing happens. And yet we must acknowledge the risk.

Key concept: Asking questions introduces personal risk.

And if we're talking about questions that point to innovation, they almost always introduce more personal risk because they challenge the status quo. They attack the way things are done. From a career standpoint, this is the high-risk, high-reward zone. Ask yourself: Are questions really welcome on my team—not soft, easy, nonthreatening questions, but courageous and disruptive questions?

Key question: Are questions welcome on your team?

Have you cultivated a culture of inquiry that is hospitable to tough, uncomfortable questions, and do people really feel that? If you want a surge of ideas, you first need a surge of questions. If you want a surge of questions, you need to nurture the highest level of psychological safety based on the respect and permission that you give people.

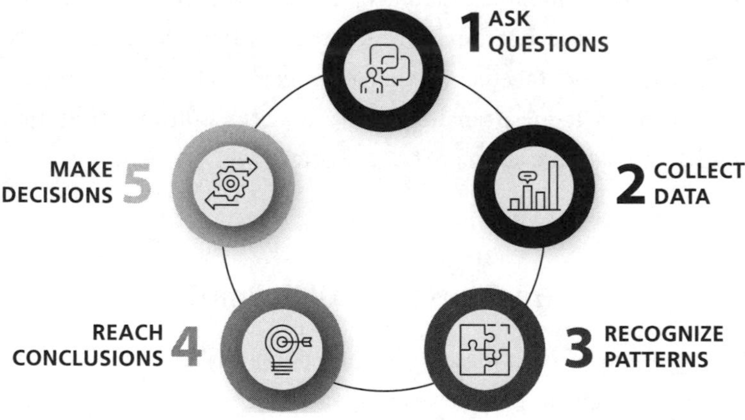

Figure 12. The process of inquiry

We see very quickly that the entire process of innovation depends on a willingness to activate the inquiry process with questions. All organizations traffic in information and ideas, but not all organizations innovate. What makes the difference? If you haven't noticed, the natural consequence of analysis is friction. People see things differently and draw different conclusions. Now comes the hard part. How do you lubricate the gears of collaboration to reduce friction? If you can do it, you'll create new value. But if the friction increases, sand becomes the lubricant and your gears will grind to a halt.

My Japanese boss was a master at nurturing a culture of inquiry. From the tone he set, I knew two things: First, there were no dumb questions. I think he had learned from experience, as many of us do, that the line between brilliance and ignorance can be very thin. Second, there were no questions that were off limits, no topics that we couldn't talk about. Those were the ground rules he established, reinforced by his own modeling behavior and a talk-to-listen ratio that hovered at fifty-fifty. Without his example and the cover he provided, I would have been reluctant to activate the inquiry process and engage in innovation. In the end, inviting questions is the spigot that turns innovation on. Discouraging questions, and punishing those who ask them, turns the spigot off.

Key concept: If you deprive your team of challenger safety, you unknowingly dedicate the team to the status quo.

Rather than protecting your team against groupthink, you're reinforcing it. You're conditioning your people not to think and not to challenge, and teams learn very quickly not to think and not to challenge. They learn very quickly how to "lock themselves inside an echo chamber of like-minded friends."[14]

Whether your team innovates and how fast your team innovates is up to you. You regulate the speed of discovery and the velocity of information. You accelerate problem-solving. You create a climate of discipline and agility. You engender the patterns and prevailing norms that allow the team to manage itself.

I worked with another CEO who needed a lot of oxygen in any room and would always commandeer meetings. He couldn't get off the stage. At the request of a distraught vice president of human resources, I attended an executive meeting with this CEO and his team to observe the dynamic. In this case, the CEO wasn't outwardly insulting, just subtly demeaning. He began the meeting and drove the agenda. He would ask yes/no questions and would become visibly agitated if his direct reports gave more than a few words of explanation beyond a simple yes or no. At one point, and I'll never forget this, the group started discussing a topic and getting into some productive dialogue. About two or three minutes in, the CEO literally opened his laptop and began doing email—in the middle of the meeting! I looked at the vice president of human resources in disbelief and she gave me a knowing look of resignation. This is the way he would censure and censor. Eventually, the CEO lost his job, dying of self-inflicted wounds: He failed because his team functioned as vertical and independent blocks of knowledge that never came together.

It's important to remember that innovation is interdisciplinary. Your success will depend, not on independent action, but on your dependent interaction. If the team can't gel and productively work through the five steps of inquiry, you'll never get there—regardless of the talent you have. You can only win as a team. It may seem unspectacular, but when you're watching innovation happen, you're watching people talk, interact, discuss, and debate. Only through that interplay and synthesis of ideas does constructive dissent, creative abrasion, and the process of combination and recombination happen.

When I was the plant manager at Geneva Steel, I learned the lifelong lesson that every system has a constraint. The constraint not only limits but also dictates the output of the entire system. The constraint is the bottleneck and other parts of the system can't compensate for it. Consider the 4-×-400-meter relay event. Each of the four members of the team runs one lap around the track. If you're the slowest member, your slowness will dictate the overall performance of the team. Everyone depends on each other. If the three other members of the team run their stages in forty-eight seconds and it takes you seventy-five, the team must still include your time in the total. Regardless of how fast they run, you're the drag.

Innovation works the same way. Your job as a leader is to reduce social friction while increasing intellectual friction. This is the primary way to de-bottleneck the innovation constraint. If you can do this, people will invest deeply in the process because they become attached to what they create through the fusion of the rational and the emotional. I see team after team exquisitely blessed with every resource it needs to innovate, except one—psychological safety, which is the constraint in the system.

Key question: What can you do to reduce the social friction on your team while increasing the intellectual friction?

It's one thing to collaborate for execution, which normally preserves the status quo. It's quite another to collaborate for innovation. Whereas execution is about creating value today, innovation is about creating value for tomorrow. It's an insurgent mission, a Skunk Works within the mothership. You're acting as disrupters in residence. That's what the great brain project is all about. The process is not tidy, clean, or linear. It's messy and iterative. Innovation is the marriage of gnarly problems and creative chaos with only a possibility that you'll produce something better.

Key concept: The pattern of innovation is to try a lot and triumph a little.

Seek Out Differences and Reduce the Risk of Ridicule

Let's dig a little deeper into the process of de-bottlenecking the organization to release its innovative potential. How do you get that innovation to flow? First, seek out differences. Second, reduce the risk of ridicule.

Remember that innovation is the process of connected people connecting things. When we say *connecting things*, we mean things that are not normally connected. For example, James Dyson, the inventor of the Dyson vacuum cleaner, said he went to a lumber yard one day and noticed giant cyclones on top of the roof that were collecting dust. Immediately, he started connecting those cyclones to his idea of a bagless vacuum. If innovation comes from connecting different things, the leader's job is to stimulate differences in the first place. Those differences become the raw material that results in innovation.[15]

You're not looking for compliance or consensus. In fact, you're looking for the opposite. You want to create and bring out differences. You want people making new, strange, and non-obvious connections. How do you do that? First, create differences in composition. That means assembling a diverse team. Diversity in composition can lead to diversity in thought. Because diversity creates dissent, diverse teams are less susceptible to groupthink.[16] Now bring out those differences by encouraging divergent thinking. Peter Drucker said, "Disagreement is needed to stimulate the imagination."[17] Again, the natural consequence of analysis is friction because people see things differently and draw different conclusions.

Key question: How do you protect your team against the dangers of groupthink?

Do you see the delicate balance? You're trying to reduce social friction, but not intellectual friction. If you have too much social friction, sand becomes the lubricant and the gears of innovation grind to a halt. If you have too little, you develop homogeneous thinking and insulate yourself, losing your ability to adapt to a changing environment. You need to nurture differences and create a theater of conflict that carries natural pressure and stress, but not fear.

My second suggestion is related to the first. When differences come out, do everything in your power as a leader to reduce the risk of ridicule. You do this by eliminating any ridiculing behavior in yourself and creating a norm that frowns on all forms of ridicule and installs peer-based accountability to maintain that norm. When it comes to innovation, challenger safety is the enabler while fear and ridicule are the inhibitors. People are born curious, so the goal is to help them stay curious. Any form of ridicule is an intellectual muzzle that shuts innovation down.

Key question: Do you feel the risk of ridicule on your team?

I remember being in a meeting with my team in which our chief financial officer openly ridiculed our chief marketing officer for some of his marketing ideas and the way he wanted to allocate his budget. Rather than intercede and call out the CFO right then and there, I let it go. I let it go in front of the entire team. I tolerated the ridicule, and my inaction that day sent a cowardly message that I spent the next month trying to undo. Because I didn't walk the talk, I opened the door for more ridicule and closed the door on more innovation. My failure of nerve compromised our challenger safety.

A team of Israeli and European social psychologists recently verified the link between psychological safety and creativity. Simply knowing that your vulnerability will not be exploited encourages you to be brave and contribute to the generative process.[18]

As the psychologist Mihaly Csikszentmihalyi argues, "Each of us is born with two contradictory sets of instructions: a conservative tendency, made up of instincts for self-preservation, self-aggrandizement, and saving energy, and an expansive tendency made up of instincts for exploring, for enjoying novelty and risk—the curiosity that leads to creativity belongs to this set."[19]

> **Key concept:** Nothing can shut down curiosity and exploratory inquiry faster than a small dose of ridicule administered at just the right time.

I've known leaders who thought it was acceptable to use ridicule for effect, perhaps reasoning that all the times they didn't use it would compensate for the few times they did. It doesn't work that way. If you scoff at an idea once for every ten times you don't, it's the scoff we remember.

> **Key concept:** The challenge with challenger safety is that it takes time to create and no time destroy.

Are You Prepared to Be Wrong?

Remember the social exchange for challenger safety: cover for candor. If your organization relies on innovation, you'll be serious about providing the needed air cover to others as they venture into the territory of challenging the status quo. You'll be more motivated to demonstrate a fundamental receptivity to both people and ideas, a cognitive and emotional openness that others clearly perceive. Not least, you'll develop the capacity to be wrong. That openness activates and facilitates the innovation process. Yes, you're a player-coach and you can participate in challenging the status quo as yourself, but your primary role is to sponsor and protect rather than snare and disinfect ideas coming from every direction.

Some leaders can't get out of their own way in this process. They net the good ideas and either cast them out or adopt them as their own. If you have an unappeasable need for status, if you crave credit and relish the trappings of power, if you need to be right, creating challenger safety may well be your biggest leadership challenge. As Oscar Munoz, the CEO of United Airlines, said, "It's the saddest thing when people haven't figured out the emotional intelligence side of things. You have to make yourself the kind of person that people are willing to come up to and provide advice."[20]

I once had a boss who wasn't very good at being wrong. He was a brazen leader with a deep sense of his own entitlement. He had a "Those who think they know everything are very offensive to those of us who do" attitude. He was dogmatic, didactic, and pedantic. It was not only tiresome to be around him, but risky. His dripping ego shut challenger safety down wherever he went. Not surprisingly, people adapted to his style quickly. One of the first adjustments his team made was to turn a real meeting into a charade. They venerated the boss with nervous respect in the official meeting, but then held the real meeting later in the form of sidebar discussions and kangaroo courts.

> **Key concept:** When a leader personally replaces the search for innovation with rivalry for prominence, the team can't achieve the social cohesion necessary for the cocreative process of innovation.

My boss was practicing territoriality by controlling the airtime—the modern version of an antiquated model of dominance that eventually sealed his fate. He was fired. The great irony about this boss was that although he was highly intelligent, he acted this way because he felt vulnerable. He didn't want to expose himself to threat or embarrassment, but in the very act of trying to give himself challenger safety, he was taking it away from us. This is exactly the pattern with a lot of smart people.[21]

You must be humble and open, and you must listen, and if you don't, the people around you will eventually have nothing to say. The world-famous cellist Yo-Yo Ma was once interviewed and asked, "What's the key to fruitful collaboration, especially across cultures or disciplines?" His response: "Ego management." In small organizations and the lower levels of large organizations, I see the pattern of hubris less often, but as you climb to the C-suite, it appears more frequently. The leadership scholar Manfred Kets de Vries asserts, "The dysfunction most frequently found at senior levels is pathological narcissism. Narcissism is not something a person either has or hasn't. We all possess narcissistic characteristics to a degree."

The speed of change outside an organization now favors the leader who explores, monitors the periphery, and extends the field of vision for the entire organization. Increasingly we will not look upon our leaders as having the answers; we will look upon them as those who can draw out those answers by tapping the creative potential of the organization.

If you have positional power, what should you do? First, know that doing all this will be difficult. Risk and fear are closely associated with formal authority. People will want to flatter you and not upset, disturb, or ruffle you. They will filter what they feed you. Make your organization culturally flat even though it's not structurally flat. Make it egalitarian. Make status an artificial constraint.

Here are three practical suggestions: First, have everyone on your team take turns conducting your regular meetings. Too many leaders monopolize that responsibility. Give everyone a turn. It will stretch them, but it will also build confidence. Second, conduct a short training segment each week and, again, rotate the responsibility to lead the training. Ensure that less experienced and lower-status individuals have the opportunity to train more experienced, higher-status individuals. This sends a clear message and accelerates development. Third, when you have a one-on-one conversation with a team member, go to them rather than have them come to you. Craig Smith will go to a student's desk and kneel next to them to help them with a calculus problem. It's a powerful gesture of servant leadership that reduces the status gap. "Wherever the barriers to the free exercise of human ingenuity were removed," the Austrian economist Friedrich August von Hayek argues, "man became rapidly able to satisfy ever widening ranges of desire."[22]

Finally, beware of the curse of success. Unfortunately, success may not be your friend when it comes to nurturing challenger safety. You've probably seen this pattern yourself: success breeds arrogance, and arrogance breeds a lack of humility, compassion, and a desire to accept feedback.[23] You may have an impressive track record due to your grit and determination, but don't let your success become a limiting factor or derailer.

Formally Assign Dissent at the Beginning

The enemy of innovation is the homogenization of thought. How will you protect against it?[24] Answer: You must assign dissent. It's not enough to model the correct behavior and informally reinforce the norms; you must formally and officially assign dissent.

Some industries have mastered this practice out of necessity because they operate in environments of high risk. For example, NASA started deploying what they called tiger teams in the 1960s. A tiger team was "a team of undomesticated and uninhibited technical specialists, selected for their experience, energy, and imagination, and assigned to track down relentlessly every possible source of failure in a spacecraft subsystem."[25] It was their job to look for potential problems, flaws, and risks. IT departments do the same thing when they commission so-called white hackers to look for vulnerabilities and potential sources of a data security breach.

Key question: Are you in the habit of formally assigning dissent to projects, initiatives, or proposed courses of action?

Finally, I've worked with many technology companies in Silicon Valley who use what they call red teams for a similar purpose. You can call it loyal opposition, playing the devil's advocate, or doing a pre-mortem. How you brand it doesn't matter. What matters is that you're formally commissioning and officially dedicating resources to vet ideas and tell you why something might not work, where it's weak, why it's flawed. Doing this provides the needed cover for candor that helps the team push through the layers of status quo bias and loss aversion that normally guard the current state. It also culturally elevates the role of dissent and makes it socially and politically acceptable.

> **Key concept:** Assigning dissent to a project, priority, or initiative from the beginning removes the natural fear normally associated with challenging the status quo.

You are not only giving people a license to challenge but also setting the expectation. In my experience, assigning dissent is the single most effective mechanism available to a leader to shift a culture toward agility. Nothing can reset cultural norms faster and more powerfully.

Conclusion

The ultimate source of adaptive capacity, competitiveness, and self-preservation, indeed the key to resilience and renewal, is the ongoing ability of an organization to learn and adapt. This capability is what allows us to engage in innovation and offer an adaptive or preemptive response. Though it may appear personally threatening, leaders must stand first in line to model the patterns of learning agility. This is not only a fundamental change from the expert model of leadership, but it also requires leaders to assume a very different emotional and social posture. Leaders will increasingly earn competence through their ability to learn and adapt rather than depending on their current knowledge and skills.

Now some final suggestions for creating challenger safety:

- Know that you are the curator of culture. You set the tone. At all costs, protect the team's right to speak up. Call anyone out that tries to silence others.
- Sometimes you will see something they can't. Sometimes they will see something you can't. If you jealously guard your own ideas, they will do the same thing. Display no pride of authorship.
- Give every member of your team the duty to disagree. Then brace yourself to hear the truth. Remember that a negative response to bad news or dissent will re-silence the team and seal your fate as a hapless leader.
- Don't make it emotionally expensive to challenge the status quo. Ask the members of your team to challenge specific things and discuss ideas on merit.
- A team often becomes lost and temporarily fails before it finds its way and eventually succeeds. This is a normal journey. The process is messy, iterative, and nonlinear, and there may be some pivots along the way. Point out that you're in uncharted territory, and help your team enjoy the journey.
- If you reject a team member's suggestion, show sensitivity by explaining why. Your considerate response will embolden the individual to keep and use their voice.[26]

Key Concepts

- Challenger safety democratizes innovation.
- When it comes to innovation, connectivity increases productivity.
- To socialize a team with challenger safety from the beginning is always easier than to re-socialize a team later.
- The social exchange for challenger safety is cover for candor.
- The more unknowns the leader eliminates through transparency, the fewer sources of stress the employee worries about.

- In the process of innovation, there is no necessary relationship between stress and fear.
- It's possible to unlock creativity in a crisis if the leader welcomes dissent and doesn't add a layer of manufactured fear to the existing level of natural stress.
- In the process of innovation, learning is more important than knowing.
- Innovation is the process of connected people connecting things.
- Asking questions introduces personal risk.
- If you deprive your team of challenger safety, you unknowingly dedicate the team to the status quo.
- The pattern of innovation is to try a lot and triumph a little.
- Nothing can shut curiosity and exploratory inquiry down faster than a small dose of ridicule administered at just the right time.
- The challenge with challenger safety is that it takes time to create and no time destroy.
- When a leader personally replaces the search for innovation with rivalry for prominence, the team can't achieve the social cohesion necessary for the co-creative process of innovation.
- Assigning dissent to a project, priority, or initiative from the beginning removes the natural fear normally associated with challenging the status quo.

Key Questions

- What patterns has your team adopted from the leader?
- Can you think of a change you started but didn't finish, where you snapped back to your original behavior?
- When was the last time you were brave and challenged the status quo?

- Do you feel that you have a license to innovate in your organization?
- When was the last time you tried to cover up a mistake? What motivated you to do that?
- Can you think of a recent example of type 1 innovation (incremental and derivative) in your organization?
- Are questions welcome on your team?
- What can you do to reduce the social friction on your team while increasing the intellectual friction?
- How do you protect your team against the dangers of groupthink?
- Do you feel the risk of ridicule on your team?
- Are you in the habit of formally assigning dissent to projects, initiatives, or proposed courses of action?

CONCLUSION

Avoiding Paternalism and Exploitation

Just remember that your real job is that
if you are free, you need to free somebody else.
If you have some power, then your job
is to empower somebody else.

—Toni Morrison

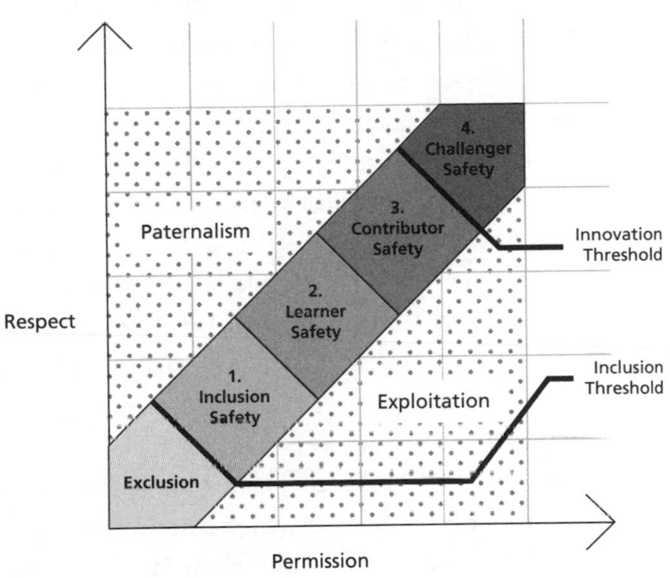

Figure 13. Dangers that appear when levels of respect and permission are low

Psychological safety requires both respect and the permission to participate. One without the other creates a dangerous imbalance that hurts people in different ways. A serious deficiency in permission pushes a team into the gutter of paternalism, whereas a serious deficiency in respect moves it into the gutter of exploitation. (See figure 13, previous page.) In either case, the organization will lack the motivation, confidence, and unit cohesion to perform at its best.

Key concept: The gutters of paternalism and exploitation flood the organization with fear.

Paternalism's lack of permission creates the fear of social isolation. When you're constantly told what to do, you get used to it, gradually becoming passive and unsure of yourself to the point that being self-reliant becomes a frightening prospect. You seek comfort more than freedom, security more than independence.

How can the social pressure to conform be stronger than the desire to express your opinions and make your own decisions?[1] Paternalism and exploitation hold the answer. Either you've been taught to be servile and compliant or you've been forced to be. I spent some time in Poland a few years after eastern Europe had been liberated. As I met with men and women and toured several manufacturing plants, the lingering Soviet influence and long night of despotism revealed itself in stubborn patterns of paternalism and exploitation that wouldn't seem to go away. Some people yielded to communist paternalism and were content to face a hopeless future. Others remained unbowed, shook off the chains of oppression, and were busy starting businesses and making things better.

In a similar way, exploitation's lack of respect creates the fear of harm in addition to the fear of isolation. Once when I was in Shanghai on business, the gentleman I was meeting with told me that he would hold confidential meetings on the street rather than in his office because he feared his office was bugged and he was being monitored under the watchful eye of government.

In both cases, paternalism and exploitation lack the balanced quantities of respect and permission that create psychological safety, leading individuals and organizations to perform below their potential. I interviewed a woman who had lived and worked under a repressive and autocratic regime in South America. "We were never allowed to be creative," she said. The patterns of paternalism and exploitation are universal, inhabiting every society and penetrating every culture. Let's take a closer look at each of these two patterns.

The Gutter of Paternalism

Paternalism is telling you what to do, supposedly in your own best interest. A higher authority will supply your needs or regulate your behavior because it doesn't believe you can do it yourself.[2] Laws are the most common form of paternalism. You must be eighteen to vote. You must wear a seatbelt. You must not swim in a riptide. These are sensible measures, but let me give you some less enlightened examples of actual laws on the books: You can't pump your own gas, can't harass Bigfoot, can't eat fried chicken except with your bare hands, can't walk backward after sunset.

We're often told that we need a benevolent parent, teacher, coach, or boss to protect us, manage our freedom, and direct our actions so we don't hurt ourselves or others, especially with fried chicken. There are certainly times when this sort of benign despotism is warranted. Remember my son who was practicing his driving to get his driver's license? He got it, and when we went to the division of motor vehicles to pick it up, the woman who issued his license made it very clear to him that his parents had the right to revoke his license at any time. The power of paternalism is often good and necessary. It protects us until we are wise enough to protect ourselves.

Key questions: Do you show signs of unnecessary paternalism toward any group or individual? Why do you do this?

Misguided paternalism means we're granting some respect to the individual but withholding the power to choose. There's a time and place for appropriate paternalism, but when it continues after the individual has demonstrated the ability to learn, contribute, or innovate without a lot of direction and guidance, it's time to back off. Not only that, it's time to listen, encourage, and empower the individual. When you're controlled by extrinsic motivation, you look outside yourself for punishments or rewards.[3] You're stripped of autonomy and, in the process, an internal impetus to action.

Key principle: Unnecessary paternalism runs the risk of breeding dependency and learned helplessness on the one hand and frustration and rebellion on the other.

Higher education, health care, and government are sectors marked by professionalism, competence, and a deep sense of collegiality. But these sectors are also more risk averse than the private sector and typically have no established norm or process for pitching or testing new ideas. They tend to hang a Do Not Disturb sign, coalesce into a "make nice" culture, and lead from the gutter of paternalism.

I've worked with many universities, health care organizations, and government agencies and consistently encounter this pattern. Health care organizations are animated by a mission to extend life and do no harm, and yet most hospitals are dominated by broken authoritarian cultures no different from the one in my steel mill. Similarly, institutions of higher learning are dedicated to the mission of education and research and are inclined to be driven by consensus. The deeply ingrained sense of respect these institutions have for humanity is beyond reproach. Where they struggle, however, is in the way they grant permission to their members to learn, participate, and most of all, innovate. Each sector is deeply entrenched in a tradition of glacial incremental change and paternalistic leadership. If you don't think paternalism is a liability in tumultuous times, consider that eighty-four nonprofit institutions of higher learning in the United States have closed their doors or been consolidated since 2016.[4]

Rather than discourage people from challenging the status quo out of fear, these sectors tend to do it through neglect. They listen to ideas, tolerate debate, express appreciation for proposed disruptive courses of action, take it all under advisement, and smile. And then not much happens. As a result, people don't self-censor out of fear; they simply leave out of frustration.

I helped with an organizational transformation with a leading research hospital that lasted a year. On both the clinical and administrative sides of the house, we spent months putting together transition plans that would take the organization from its current state to a better one. We had long-term strategic plans, shorter-term tactical plans, and even shorter-term operational plans that included assignments, due dates, and other details. After all this preparation, the executive team came back and said, "We just don't think the organization is quite ready for the transition. We're going to think about doing it next year."

What this hospital had learned is the lesson that most paternalistic leaders eventually learn: Paternalism is safe in the short term but grows dangerous in the long term. In your benevolence, you cut off the circulation of local knowledge that is flowing to you from the bottom of the organization, suffer the consequences of isolation, and find yourself in crisis later.

Health care, higher education, and government are good examples of paternalism, but it exists in every industry and sector. In most paternalistic societies, there's strong deference to authority and a desire to honor the past. People try to say yes to every request because they don't want to appear disloyal. Saying no is an unpopular answer, and no one wants to face social disapproval. Over time, paternalism leads to a low tolerance for candor and a lack of bravery. If the pattern becomes widely and deeply institutionalized, it compounds risk and often explodes in crisis.

Except for natural disasters, nearly every human crisis announces itself in advance. In paternalistic organizations, the warnings often go unheeded. Scandals and business failures don't come out of nowhere. Why would an organization repeatedly choose not to respond to early warning signs? Agile, alert organizations respond. Lumbering paternalistic ones don't.

The Gutter of Exploitation

Exploitation combines high permission with low respect. It tends to be motivated by the universal temptation toward despotism—the urge to control others for gain and gratification.

> **Key concept:** Whether personal or organizational, exploitation requires some type of repressive apparatus by which to extract value from humans, either by manipulation or coercion.

Exploitation comes in degrees but it is always based on the exploiter's allegiance to selfish ambition. James Madison reminded us in the *Federalist Paper 10* that "enlightened statesmen will not always be at the helm." Think of Jack Ma, the founder of China's internet giant, Alibaba, and his promotion of what he calls the 996 work schedule: you work from 9 a.m. to 9 p.m., six days a week, with no overtime pay. Isn't it interesting that he frames it as a "philosophy" to give it more legitimacy? Similarly, my nephew recently finished a stint at a major investment bank and was required to work from 6 a.m. to 9 p.m. every day. Is there any concern for the needs of human beings in this case? No, it's the pure extraction of utility. The asymmetry in the way value is created and captured is the dead giveaway. When acquisition becomes an addiction, corporate chieftains tune their organizations based on a pure shareholder-return theory of the corporation.[5] That's the beginning and the end of their stewardship, which often leads to predatory tendencies toward employees.

What concerns me is that people can become conditioned to accept exploitation, which leads to the normalization of abuse. Reflect on these words from the great Russian novelist Alexander Solzhenitsyn, "Peasants are a silent people, without a literary voice, nor do they write complaints or memoirs."[6] He may have been talking about another time and place, but the pattern is the same: When exploitation is permitted, people learn to accept it without complaint. Even those who are exploited can become defenders of the very exploitation they suffer. What makes it confusing, and therefore sustains it, is when leaders alternate acts of kindness and generosity with acts of violence and abuse.

> **Key concept:** Exploitation is the process of extracting value from another human being while disregarding that person's inherent value.

In civil society, most forms of coercive exploitation are illegal and therefore less visible. Ironically, we have officially purged civil society of slavery, and yet human trafficking is at an all-time high, with an estimated forty million persons working in forced labor and servitude. But the most common forms of exploitation are not illegal, just immoral. They take the form of rudeness, unkindness, incivility, and abuse, and they exact a terrifying toll. Christine Porath and Christine Pearson, for example, show in their research that 98 percent of workers have experienced uncivil behavior at work. Half report being treated rudely at work at least once a week.[7]

> **Key questions:** Do you show signs of exploitation toward any group or individual? Why do you do this?

Beware the Land of False Fellowship

I said in the preface that human beings long to belong. But that longing can be taken too far. When others prey on your need to belong, there comes a point when you must say adios, when it's far better to live without approval because that approval is feigned and destructive. As the philosopher Terry Warner has rightly observed, "Approval is held out as relief from this insecurity."[8] At some point, we simply need to stop caring about what others think. If not, we become vulnerable to further exploitation, giving others the power to control or manipulate us, and turning us into victims. Social approval, belonging, and connectedness are needs. But no one really needs constant validation. If your most consuming fear is to be alone, you're easy prey to a shaming culture, and you would do well to pry yourself away from the social mirror. In the digital world, to be happy in your own company is a survival skill. When necessary, healthy rejection of popular opinion is a beautiful thing.

> **Key concept:** We crave attention, sometimes even if it's the wrong kind. Attention alone never satisfies, but it can deeply hurt.

My son came home from middle school one day and was talking about how many followers his friends had on Instagram. He then proceeded to tell me that several of them use their parents' credit cards to purchase followers. If that were not alarming enough, he said some of the parents encourage it. The like button has become an altar of worship.

If you want to be happy, you will sometimes need to politely disconnect to protect yourself. Anyone who thinks that their inherent worth will diminish if they don't have constant validation from others doesn't understand the meaning of *inherent*.[9]

Many people stand ready to shame you if you don't join their ranks, do what they do, think what they think, or wear what they wear. If your happiness depends on popular opinion, prepare to be unhappy.

A shaming culture demands compliance and hurls contempt on those who dare leave its company. In such a place, relationships are based on the reciprocation of flattery and false praise. In this self-imposed reality-distortion field, we breathe fiction to our neighbors, and they to us. We feed on appearance and image and drink the strong wine of self-deceit. If you live or work in such a congress of cowards, please remember that humans have always created social units where anyone is welcome, admission is free, but the truth is forbidden. You can be anyone you want to be except your true and authentic self.

In the land of false fellowship, members gain their sense of identity from the common sense of superiority they feel for themselves and the common sense of disdain they feel for others. Relationships are superficial and loyalty conditional. People enter those relationships to deflect the truth about themselves.

Key concept: In the land of false fellowship, unnatural competition replaces natural affection.

But what if you're already in the land of false fellowship? What if you're in a relationship you need to escape, enduring abusive treatment, tolerating destructive behavior? What do you do? First, understand that the other party will often try to convince you that you need them or that you must accept their treatment. Prepare for skillful manipulation. The control response is as predictable as the sunrise. As the Eagles' song goes, "You can check out anytime you like. But you can never leave."[10] The truth is, you can leave.

If you're being exploited, abused, or harassed, you're being denied the respect and permission you're entitled to as a human being. If that's not going to change, give yourself inclusion safety. Sometimes that means standing alone, absorbing an economic loss, being misunderstood, or taking a hit to your reputation. In my own professional life, I've witnessed psychological terrorism at its worst and watched it demolish self-worth and drown initiative and creativity. I've worked with business associates who have been driven by greed and unbridled ambition and think it no crime to leave a wake of economic and emotional destruction behind them. There have been times when

I was too trusting and didn't acknowledge the warning signs of ulterior motive and ill intent. We've all been scraped by an insecure leader, a cruel pretender, a small-time exploiter on the take. Sooner or later, we find ourselves swimming in a red zone, on the receiving end of hurt and humiliation.

As fellow travelers, we scrape each other. As I said in the preface, we're all wounded and guilty. But when the hurt comes deliberately and continually, that's abuse. It's time to create boundaries and change the terms of engagement. I can't possibly address the vast ocean of human suffering, and I fully understand the threat of real danger. In my volunteer work, I've helped abuse victims in tragic circumstances and seen the wreckage that surrounds them. In the end, we can and must help ourselves.

Nobody is a nobody. Whether or not you're accepted, you're acceptable. If you're human, you're enough. But you must act to protect yourself. Here are some suggestions:

- Love yourself first. Give yourself inclusion safety—the respect and permission you inherently deserve. If others won't give you psychological safety, you must at least give it to yourself as you work to change your circumstances.
- Be alert to the motives of those around you. If you observe others acting maliciously toward you, even if it's mild, act early to confront the behavior or remove yourself from the situation.
- Don't believe that you must accept abusive treatment. That's a lie. Do everything in your power to protect yourself.
- Learn resilience in your resistance. As you work to liberate yourself from unhealthy treatment, fight back in healthy ways. Because of the hurt, anger, guilt, self-hatred, and anguish people suffer as a result of social and emotional persecution, they often resort to equally unhealthy response patterns. That just makes things worse. Avoid drugs and all forms of self-harm and self-indulgence. Don't heap more hurt on yourself.

- If you feel dominated, controlled, or trapped, with no apparent means of escape, search for a way out or leave immediately. In the meantime, refuse to entertain damaging thoughts about yourself. You can eventually heal and overcome everything.
- Find and connect with trustworthy, happy people who genuinely want your success and are willing to help. Consult with them as you make decisions and consider options.

Key question: Have you ever felt trapped in the land of false fellowship? How long did you stay? How did you get out?

Sixty Billion Interactions Every Day

The world's population is fast approaching eight billion. Every day those nearly eight billion people have an estimated sixty billion interactions with each other. In each interaction we extend a measure of respect and permission, which determines a certain level of psychological safety. Each one of those interactions either nourishes or neglects human potential.

The more we create psychological safety, the more we enjoy the rewards of rich connection, belonging, and collaboration. The less we create it, the more we suffer the bitterness and sting of isolation.

We seem to be stuck in an existential fog in which the complex social matrix in which we live our lives is our biggest challenge. We alone are responsible for the antagonisms we create among ourselves, and yet we continue to shed emotional blood, not just occasionally, but constantly. Are we medieval? Have we not ripened in wisdom?

Psychological safety is built on a moral foundation of looking on our fellow creatures with respect and giving them permission to belong and contribute. That isn't to say that we condone flagrant or harmful ethical misconduct, or that we don't judge the skill and performance of each other. We must do that. We're all accountable. But when it comes to worth, people are owed respect because they're people. The moment we begin to devalue, objectify, or dehumanize each other, we forsake humanity. Don't tell me you have a company to run or results to deliver. Don't tell me you're important. Don't tell me this is high stakes, or you're under pressure, or you have your triggers, or you're prone to grown-up meltdowns. If you make any excuse for not extending psychological safety, you're choosing to value something else more than human beings. Consider, for example, the thirty-five employees at France Télécom who recently took their own lives as a result of relentless and systematic harassment.[11] Rather than creating a supportive, humanistic workplace, the leaders dehumanized their lower-ranking colleagues with institutionalized oppression, leading to tragic consequences.

We can give ourselves warm baths of self-satisfaction and blame our poor behavior on personality, work style, pressure, stress, anxiety, deadlines, or a disadvantaged past. Welcome to the human race. We don't get a pass for those things. Remember, we can't claim special status. But isn't that what we're doing when we refuse to extend psychological safety to another person? So is hiding behind the guise of tolerance or political correctness only to excoriate those who don't share our values or agenda.

Harvard's seventy-five-year study of human happiness, which is now in its fourth generation, has identified what we already know intuitively: As the grant study's director, Robert Waldinger, summarizes, "The clearest message that we get from this 75-year study is this: Good relationships keep us happier and healthier."[12] It's connection that in the end brings us sustained happiness. With its restorative and healing powers, cultivating relationships is the one nonpharmaceutical therapy, the one redemptive act, that continues to bring us the most joy.

A Swelling Demand for Leaders Who Create Psychological Safety

When I say the words *human potential*, what comes to mind? Think about the potential of those around you—your family, friends, neighbors, classmates, coworkers. Ironically, whether you care about their potential or not, you have an impact on it, and others have a profound impact on yours. The people you spend the most time with are the ones you influence the most. But even those you rarely see, even those with whom you may have had only a chance encounter, may be profoundly affected by your influence. Even a few words can change a life. Through our interactions we cultivate or crush potential. Which always brings us back to the concept of psychological safety.

In the days ahead, you will see a swelling demand for leaders who create a high level of psychological safety on their teams and in their organizations. This demand is the natural consequence of competing in a highly dynamic environment that relies on constant innovation. It's also the natural consequence of highly intelligent people who've had one too many bosses dripping with ego and control issues.

Key concept: At an individual level, we need personal fulfillment and happiness. At an organizational level, we need innovation and a sustained competitive advantage.

In fact, we're starting to see the beginning of a sea change in how many of the best organizations in the world choose their leaders. It's counterintuitive to the conventional thinking that a leader must be a charismatic, hard-driving repository of vision and answers. In fact, the traditional archetype of a leader, forged on the imperial concept of leadership, abundant with hubris and advocacy skills, is fast becoming an occupational hazard. The primary characteristic of this new variety is an individual who possesses superb emotional intelligence with a highly controlled ego.

Key question: Do you practice the imperial concept of leadership, or have you evolved to a higher stage of development based on emotional intelligence and controlled ego?

A growing body of research confirms that emotional intelligence creates psychological safety in the organization, which, as a mediating variable, accelerates innovation. In hypercompetitive markets, innovation is the lifeblood of survival and the mainspring of growth. Thus, the leader of the twenty-first century must be able to thrive in this context as an example of collaboration, creative abrasion, and humility.

The industrial concepts of command and control on the one hand and benevolent paternalism on the other are dying an ignominious death because they activate the self-censoring instinct and shut down the ability to innovate. If we don't cultivate a higher tolerance for candor, we can't convince people to release their discretionary efforts. They're already hypervigilant to any threat. So the single most important question in the selection of a leader is fast becoming this: Does the individual create or destroy psychological safety and therefore stimulate or stifle innovation? In a letter to employees, Satya Nadella, the CEO of Microsoft, expressed the spirit of psychological safety and the path to inclusion and innovation: "Together, we must embrace our shared humanity, and aspire to create a society that is filled with respect, empathy, and opportunity for all."[13]

Pluralism is our reality. In our hierarchy of loyalties, let's think above personal and tribal differences and enshrine our central tie, the allegiance and affinity that matters most: the bond of belonging to the human family.

Let me return to the call to action I issued at the beginning of the book. I invited you to conduct a searching personal inventory about the way you behave toward others, especially those who are strangers or against whom you have a lingering bias or prejudice.

1. **Inclusion safety:** Are you prepared to cross the threshold of inclusion, bridge differences, and invite others into your society?
2. **Learner safety:** Are you prepared to encourage others to learn?
3. **Contributor safety:** Are you prepared to give others the autonomy to contribute and deliver results?
4. **Challenger safety:** And finally, are you prepared to cross the threshold of innovation and provide air cover for others to challenge the status quo and innovate?

To conclude, let me share an ancient case study in psychological safety. Regardless of your religious persuasion, the story is awesomely powerful. In the New Testament, in the book of Acts, Peter, a Jew, is taken to Cornelius, a Roman centurion. Peter had grown up with the understanding that non-Jews were common or unclean. He had lived his entire life in a segregated society based on this paradigm and prejudice. Yet when Peter encounters Cornelius, he says, "Ye know how that it is an unlawful thing for a man that is a Jew to keep company, or come unto one of another nation; but God hath shewed me that I should not call any man common or unclean."[14]

Alexander the Great famously remarked that there were "no more worlds to conquer." There is at least one—the inclination to conquer each other.

The greatest source of fulfillment in life comes from including others, helping them learn and grow, unleashing their potential, and finding deep communion together. That's the lesson. Now look around and see others with fresh amazement.

Key Concepts

- The gutters of paternalism and exploitation flood the organization with fear.

- Paternalism runs the risk of breeding dependency and learned helplessness on the one hand and frustration and rebellion on the other.
- Whether personal or organizational in nature, exploitation requires some type of repressive apparatus by which to extract value from humans, either by manipulation or coercion.
- Exploitation is the process of extracting value from another human being while disregarding that person's inherent value.
- We crave attention, sometimes even if it's the wrong kind. Attention alone never satisfies, but it can deeply hurt.
- In the land of false fellowship, unnatural competition replaces natural affection.
- At an individual level, we need personal fulfillment and happiness. At an organizational level, we need innovation and sustained competitive advantage.

Key Questions

- Have you ever felt trapped in the land of false fellowship? How long did you stay? How did you get out?
- Do you show signs of paternalism toward any group or individual? Why do you do this?
- Do you show signs of exploitation toward any group or individual? Why do you do this?
- Do you practice the imperial concept of leadership or have you evolved to a higher stage of development based on emotional intelligence and controlled ego?

Notes

Preface

1. As a newcomer, my experience was overflowing with change, contrast, and surprises of all kinds. See Louis, Meryl Reis. "Surprise and Sense Making: What Newcomers Experience in Entering Unfamiliar Organizational Settings." *Administrative Science Quarterly* 25, no. 2 (1980): 226–51.

2. C. Wright Mills, *The Power Elite*, new edition (New York: Oxford University Press, 1956, 2000), 9.

3. Robert Conquest, *History, Humanity, and Truth: The Jefferson Lecture in the Humanities* (Stanford, CA: Hoover Press, 1993), 7.

4. Immanuel Kant made the precursor argument that civil freedom enables intellectual freedom. See *Kant: Political Writings*, Hans Reiss, ed., Cambridge: Cambridge University Press, 2010, p. 59)

5. Moyers & Company, "Facing Evil with Maya Angelou," September 13, 2014, video, 31:00, https://archive.org/details/KCSM_20140914_020000_Moyers __Company/start/0/end/60.

6. Jake Herway, "How to Create a Culture of Psychological Safety," *Workplace*, December 7, 2017, http://news.gallup.com/opinion/gallup/223235/create-culture psychological-safety.aspx.

7. Langston Hughes, *Selected Poems of Langston Hughes* (New York: Vintage Classics, 1959), 20.

8. Hannah Arendt, *Men in Dark Times* (New York: Harcourt Brace, 1993), 4.

9. Thomas Hobbes, *Leviathan*, in *The Harvard Classics: French and English Philosophers: Descartes, Rousseau, Voltaire, Hobbes*, ed. Charles W. Eliot (New York: F. F. Collier & Son, 1910), 385.

10. Rowan Williams, address to Wheaton College Theology Conference, April 6, 2018, video, 49:13, https://www.youtube.com/watch?v=R58Q_Q3KEnM.

11. Matthew Stewart, "The 9.9 Percent Is the New American Aristocracy," *The Atlantic*, June 2018, https://www.theatlantic.com/magazine/archive/2018/06/the -birth-of-a-new-american-aristocracy/559130/.

12. See W. B. Yeats, "The Circus Animal's Desertion."

Introduction

1. See, for example, Amy Edmondson, "Psychological Safety and Learning Behavior in Work Teams," *Administrative Science Quarterly* 44, no. 2 (June 1999): 350–383, http://web.mit.edu/curhan/www/docs/Articles/15341_Readings/Group_Performance/Edmondson%20Psychological%20safety.pdf. For a useful review of the psychological safety literature, see Alexander Newman, Ross Donohue, Nathan Evans, "Psychological Safety: A Systematic Review of the Literature," *Human Resource Management Review* 27, no. 3 (September 2017): 521–535, https://www.sciencedirect.com/science/article/abs/pii/S1053482217300013; Amy C. Edmondson and Zhike Lei, "Psychological Safety: The History, Renaissance, and Future of an Interpersonal Construct," *Annual Review of Organizational Psychology and Organizational Behavior* 1 (March 2014): 23–43; William A. Kahn, "Psychological Conditions of Personal Engagement and Disengagement at Work," *The Academy of Management Journal* 33, no. 4 (December 1990): 692–724.

2. Carl R. Rogers, "The Necessary and Sufficient Conditions of Therapeutic Personality Change," *Journal of Consulting Psychology* 21 (1957): 95–103.

3. Douglas McGregor, *The Human Side of Enterprise* (New York: McGraw-Hill, 1960), 37. Here's the full quote: "When a man's physiological needs are satisfied and he is no longer fearful about his physical welfare, his social needs become important motivators of his behavior. These are such needs as those for belonging, for association, for acceptance by one's fellows, for giving and receiving love."

4. Herbert A. Simon, *Administrative Behavior* (New York: The Free Press, 1997), 214.

5. Abraham H. Maslow, "A Theory of Human Motivation," *Psychological Review* 50 (1943): 380.

6. See chap. 1 in Eric Fromm, *Escape from Freedom* (New York: Holt, Rineholt and Winston, 1941).

7. Arlie Russell Hochschild, *The Managed Heart: Commercialization of Human Feeling*. (Berkeley: University of California Press, 1983), 56.

8. See Charles Duhigg, "What Google Learned from Its Quest to Build the Perfect Team," *New York Times*, February 25, 2016, https://www.nytimes.com/2016/02/28/magazine/what-google-learned-from-its-quest-to-build-the-perfect-team.html. See also Google's Project Aristotle, accessed August 1, 2019, https://rework.withgoogle.com/print/guides/5721312655835136/.

9. Celia Swanson, "Are You Enabling a Toxic Culture Without Realizing It?" *Harvard Business Review*, August 22, 2019. https://hbr.org/2019/08/are-you-enabling-a-toxic-culture-without-realizing-it.

10. American College Health Association, "National College Health Assessment Executive Summary," Fall 2017, https://www.acha.org/documents/ncha/NCHA-II_FALL_2017_REFERENCE_GROUP_EXECUTIVE_SUMMARY.pdf.

11. See Marshall Sahlins, "The Original Affluent Society" (abridged) in *The Politics of Egalitarianism: Theory and Practice,* ed. Jacqueline Solway (New York: Berghahn Books, 2006), 78–98.

12. William James, *The Principles of Psychology* (Boston, 1890).

13. Holly Hedegaard, Sally C. Curtin, and Margaret Warner, *Suicide Mortality in the United States, 1999–2017,* NCHS data brief no. 330 (Hyattsville, MD: National Center for Health Statistics, Centers for Disease Control, November 2018), https://www.cdc.gov/nchs/data/databriefs/db330-h.pdf.

14. Albert Camus in *More Letters of Note: Correspondence Deserving of a Wider Audience,* compiled by Shaun Usher (Edinburgh: Canongate and Unbound, 2017), 279.

15. Paul Petrone, "The Skills Companies Need Most in 2019," *LinkedIn Learning,* accessed August 1, 2019, https://learning.linkedin.com/blog/top-skills/the-skills-companies-need-most-in-2019--and-how-to-learn-them.

16. Rita Gunther McGrath, "Five Ways to Ruin Your Innovation Process," *Harvard Business* Review, June 5, 2012, https://hbr.org/2012/06/five-ways-to-ruin-your-inno.

17. Scott D. Anthony et al., "2018 Corporate Longevity Forecast: Creative Destruction Is Accelerating," *Innosight,* 2018, 2. https://www.innosight.com/wp-content/uploads/2017/11/Innosight-Corporate-Longevity-2018.pdf.

Stage 1: Inclusion Safety

1. *The Impact of Equality and Values Driven Business*, Salesforce Research, 12, accessed August 5, 2019, https://c1.sfdcstatic.com/content/dam/web/en_us/www/assets/pdf/datasheets/salesforce-research-2017-workplace-equality-and-values-report.pdf.

2. See William Law, *A Serious Call to a Devout and Holy Life* (n.p.: ReadaClassic, 2010), 244. Law underscores the point that "there is no dependence upon the merits of men."

3. See Amartya Sen, *Identity and Violence: The Illusion of Destiny* (New York: W. W. Norton, 2006), 2–3.

4. John Winthrop, "A Model of Christian Charity," a sermon delivered in April 1630 to the pilgrims traveling to the Massachusetts Bay Colony.

5. John Rawls, *A Theory of Justice* (Oxford: Oxford University Press, 1972), 5.

6. And it's what we would all choose if we had to define the "original position" behind a "veil of ignorance," as Rawls describes his thought experiment.

7. Jia Hu et al., "Leader Humility and Team Creativity: The Role of Team Information Sharing, Psychological Safety, and Power Distance," *Journal of Applied Psychology* 103, no. 3 (2018): 313–323.

8. Henry Emerson Fosdick, *The Meaning of Service* (New York: Association Press, 1944), 138.

9. See Isaiah Berlin, *Concepts and Categories: Philosophical Essays* (Oxford: Oxford University Press, 1980), 96.

10. Alex "Sandy" Pentland, "The New Science of Building Great Teams," *Harvard Business Review*, April 2012, https://hbr.org/2012/04/the-new-science-of-building-great-teams.

11. Edgar Schein, *Organizational Culture and Leadership* (San Francisco: Jossey-Bass, 2004), 15.

12. Vaclav Havel, *The Power of the Powerless* (New York: Vintage Classics, 2018), iv.

13. Aristotle, *The Politics of Aristotle*, vol. 1, trans. B. Jowett (Oxford: Clarendon Press, 1885), 3.

14. David McCullough, *John Adams* (New York: Simon & Schuster, 2001), 170.

15. Thomas Jefferson himself believed in his own biological superiority. See *Notes on the State of Virginia*, 1781, accessed August 1, 2019, https://docsouth.unc.edu/southlit/jefferson/jefferson.html.

16. EY, "Could Trust Cost You a Generation of Talent," accessed August 9, 2019, https://www.ey.com/Publication/vwLUAssets/ey-could-trust-cost-you-a-generation-of-talent/%24FILE/ey-could-trust-cost-you-a-generation-of-talent.pdf.

17. Robert Putnam, *Bowling Alone: The Collapse and Revival of American Community* (New York: Simon & Schuster, 2000), 21.

18. Ferdinand Tönnies, *Gemeinschaft und Gesellschaft* (Leipzig, Germany: Fues's Verlag, 1887). An English translation of the 8th edition (1935) by Charles P. Loomis appeared as *Fundamental Concepts of Sociology* (New York: American Book Co., 1940).

19. James MacGregor Burns, *Leadership* (New York: Perennial, 1978), 11.

20. Carol Dweck, *Mindset: The New Psychology of Success* (New York: Random House, 2006), 121.

21. Franz Kafka, *Letters to Friend, Family, and Editors*, Richard and Clara Winston, editors, (New York: Schoken Books, 1977), 16.

22. Nathaniel Branden, *The Six Pillars of Self-Esteem* (Bantam: New York, 1994), 7.

23. See Edward H. Chang et al., "The Mixed Effects of Online Diversity Training," *Proceedings of the National Academy of Sciences*, 116, no. 16 (April 16, 2019): 7778–7783; first published April 1, 2019, https://doi.org/10.1073/pnas.1816076116.

24. Paul Ekman and Richard J. Davidson, "Voluntary Smiling Changes Regional Brain Activity," *Psychological Science* 4, no. 5 (September 1993): 342–45, https://doi.org/10.1111/j.1467-9280.1993.tb00576.x.

25. See Oscar Peterson, "Hymn to Freedom," whose lyrics say, "When every heart joins every heart and together yearns for liberty, that's when we'll be free."

Stage 2: Learner Safety

1. Tony Miller, "Partnering for Education Reform," U.S. Department of Education, accessed February 18, 2015, https://www.ed.gov/news/speeches/partnering-education-reform.

2. See James. J. Heckman, "Catch'em Young," *Wall Street Journal*, January 6, 2006. https://www.wsj.com/articles/SB113686119611542381.

3. Robert Balfanz and Nettie Legters, *Locating the Dropout Crisis* (Baltimore: Center for Research on the Education of Students Placed at Risk, Johns Hopkins University, September 2004), accessed August 1, 2019, https://files.eric.ed.gov/fulltext/ED484525.pdf.

4. This section draws heavily on my personal interviews with Craig from 2014 to 2019 as well as classroom observations conducted in 2019. Disclosure: Craig has taught five of my children in his calculus classes.

5. Why, for example, are females dramatically underrepresented in computer science and STEM majors in college? Undoubtedly, part of the gap is due to an unconscious bias that says they can't excel as well as males can in these fields even though they perform as well as males in K-12 standardized math tests and earn 57 percent of bachelor's degrees today. See Thomas Dee and Seth Gershenson, Unconscious Bias in the Classroom: Evidence and Opportunities (Mountain View, CA: Google's Computer Science Education Research, 2017), accessed August 1, 2019, https://goo.gl/06Btqi. See also David M. Amodio, "The Neuroscience of Prejudice and Stereotyping," *Nature Reviews Neuroscience* 15, no. 10 (2014): 670–682.

6. Jenna McGregor, "Nobel Prize-Winning Psychologist to CEOs: Don't Be So Quick to Go with Your Gut," *Washington Post*, March 4, 2019, https://www.washingtonpost.com/business/2019/03/04/nobel-prize-winning-psychologist-ceos-dont-be-so-quick-go-with-your-gut/?utm_term=.b1cfde227f5e.

7. C. Roland Christensen, *Education for Judgment*, (Boston: Harvard Business Review, 1991), 118.

8. Claude M. Steele, *Whistling Vivaldi: How Stereotypes Affect Us and What We Can Do* (New York: W. W. Norton & Co., 2010), 46.

9. From classroom observation conducted on February 14, 2019.

10. See Jenny W. Rudolph, Daniel B. Raemer, and Robert Simon, "Establishing a Safe Container for Learning in Simulation: The Role of the Presimuation Briefing," *Journal of the Society for Simulation in Healthcare* 9, no. 6 (December 2014): 339–349. Smith's classroom becomes the safe container.

11. See Ernest Hemingway's short story "A Clean, Well-Lighted Place." Craig's practices embody the primary findings released in the Aspen Institute's national report *A Nation at Hope*, accessed March 12, 2019, http://nationathope.org/.

12. C. Roland Christensen, "Premises and Practices of Discussion Teaching," in *Education for Judgment: The Artistry of Discussion Leadership*, C. Roland Christensen and David A. Garvin, eds. (Boston: Harvard Business Review, 1991), 15–34.

13. Babette Bronkhorst, "Behaving Safely under Pressure: The Effects of Job Demands, Resources, and Safety Climate on Employee Physical and Psychosocial Safety Behavior," *Journal of Safety Research* 55 (December 2015): 63–72.

14. *Fast Company,* "Bill Gates on Education: 'We Can Make Massive Strides,'" April 15, 2013, https://www.fastcompany.com/3007841/bill-gates-education-we-can-make-massive-strides.

15. Education World, "How Can Teachers Develop Students' Motivation and Success: Interview with Carol Dweck, accessed August 10, 2019, https://www.educationworld.com/a_issues/chat/chat010.shtml.

16. Richard Florida, *The Rise of the Creative Class* (New York: Basic Books, 2002), 24.

17. Malcolm S. Knowles, "Adult Learning" in *The ASTD Training and Development Handbook: A Guide to Human Resource Development*, Robert L. Craig, ed., 4th ed. (New York: McGraw-Hill, 2004), 262.

18. Amy C. Edmondson. "Making It Safe: The Effects of Leader Inclusiveness and Professional Status on Psychological Safety and Improvement Efforts in Health Care Teams," *Journal of Organizational Behavior* 27, no. 7 (2006): 941–966.

19. See Roderick M. Kramer and Karen S. Cook, eds., *Trust and Distrust in Organizations: Dilemmas and Approaches* (New York: Russell Sage Foundation, 2004).

Stage 3: Contributor Safety

1. Vincent H. Dominé, "Team Development in the Era of Slack," *INSEAD Knowledge*, May 24, 2019, https://knowledge.insead.edu/blog/insead-blog/team-development-in-the-era-of-slack-11611.

2. See Claude M. Steele and Joshua Aronson, "Stereotype Threat and the Intellectual Test Performance of African Americans," *Journal of Personality and Social Psychology* 69, no. 5 (November 1995): 797–811.

3. See Steven R. Harper and Charles D. White, "The Impact of Member Emotional Intelligence on Psychological Safety in Work Teams," *Journal of Behavioral & Applied Management* 15, no. 1 (2013): 2–10.

4. Amy Edmondson, *The Fearless Organization: Creating Psychological Safety in the Workplace for Learning, Innovation, and Growth* (New York: Wiley, 2019), chap. 4.

5. See Christopher J. Roussin et al., "Psychological Safety, Self-Efficacy, and Speaking Up in Interprofessional Health Care Simulation," *Clinical Simulation in Nursing* 17 (April 2018): 38–46.

6. Jim Harter, "Dismal Employee Engagement Is a Sign of Global Mismanagement," *Gallup Workplace*, accessed August 1, 2019, https://www.gallup.com/workplace/231668/dismal-employee-engagement-sign-global-mismanagement.aspx.

7. Aristotle, *The Nicomachean Ethics*, in *The Complete Works of Aristotle: The Revised Oxford Translation*, ed. Jonathan Barnes, rev. by J. O. Urmson Ross, vol. 2 (Oxford University Press, 1984), 1107.

Stage 4: Challenger Safety

1. See Carl R. Rogers and F. J. Roethlisberger, "Barriers and Gateways to Communication." *Harvard Business Review*, November-December 1991, https://hbr.org/1991/11/barriers-and-gateways-to-communication.

2. Marcus Du Sautoy, *The Creativity Code: Art and Innovation in the Age of AI* (Cambridge, MA: Belknap Press, 2019), 11.

3. Edward O. Wilson, *The Origins of Creativity* (New York: Liveright publishers, 2017), 1.

4. Ben Farr-Wharton and Ace Simpson, "Human-centric Models of Management Are the Key to Ongoing Success," *The Sydney Morning Herald*, May 24, 2019, https://www.smh.com.au/business/workplace/human-centric-models-of-management-are-the-key-to-ongoing-success-20190520-p51p82.html.

5. Edgar Schein, *Humble Inquiry* (San Francisco: Berrett-Koehler, 2013), 64.

6. Chris Argyris, "Good Communication That Blocks Learning," *Harvard Business Review*, July-August 1994, https://hbr.org/1994/07/good-communication-that-blocks-learning.

6. Chia Nakane, *Japanese Society* (Berkeley: University of California Press, 1972), 13.

8. Abraham Carmeli et al., "Learning Behaviors in the Workplace: The Role of High-Quality Interpersonal Relationships and Psychological Safety," *Systems Research and Behavioral Science* 26, no. 25 (November 2008): 81–98.

9. Abraham Maslow, "Safe Enough to Dare," in *Toward a Psychology of Being*, 3rd ed. (New York: Wiley, 1998), 65.

10. Duena Blostrom, "Nobody Gets Fired for Buying IBM, but They Should," blog post, January 1, 2019, https://duenablomstrom.com/2019/01/01/nobody-gets-fired-for-buying-ibm-but-they-should/.

11. Andrew Hargadon and Robert I. Sutton, "Building an Innovation Factory," *Harvard Business Review*, May–June 2000, https://hbr.org/2000/05/building-an-innovation-factory-2.

12. Adam Lashinsky, "The Unexpected Management Genius of Facebook's Mark Zuckerberg," *Fortune*, November 10, 2016, accessed August 11, 2019, https://fortune.com/longform/facebook-mark-zuckerberg-business/.

13. Alison Beard, "Life's Work: An Interview with Brian Wilson," *Harvard Business Review*, December 2016, accessed August 11, 2019, https://hbr.org/2016/12/brian-wilson.

14. Yuval Noah Harari, *21 Lessons for the 21st Century* (New York: Spiegel & Grau, 2018), 223.

15. Jeff Dyer, Hal Gregersen, and Clayton M. Christensen, *The Innovator's DNA: Mastering the Five Skills of Disruptive Innovators* (Boston: Harvard Business School Press, 2011), 46–49.

16. Vivian Hunt, Dennis Layton, and Sara Prince, *Diversity Matters* (New York: McKinsey & Company, February 2, 2015), 14, https://assets.mckinsey.com/~/media/857F440109AA4D13A54D9C496D86ED58.ashx.

17. Peter F. Drucker, *The Effective Executive* (New York: Harper Business, 1996), 152.

18. Dotan R. Castro et al., "Mere Listening Effect on Creativity and the Mediating Role of Psychological Safety," *Psychology of Aesthetics, Creativity, and the Arts* 12, no. 4 (November 2018): 489–502.

19. Mihaly Csikszentmihalyi, *Creativity: Flow and the Psychology of Discovery and Invention* (New York: Harper Perennial, 1997), 11.

20. Jennifer Luna, "Oscar Munoz: Learn to Listen, Improve Your EQ," *Stanford Business*, January 19, 2019, https://www.gsb.stanford.edu/insights/oscar-munoz-learn-listen-improve-your-eq?utm_source=Stanford+Business&utm_campaign=44021e6e06-Stanford-Business-Issue-154-1-27-2018&utm_medium=email&utm_term=0_0b5214e34b-44021e6e06-74101045&ct=t (Stanford-Business-Issue-154-1-27-2018).

21. Chris Argyris, "Teaching Smart People How to Learn," *Harvard Business Review*, May-June 1991, https://hbr.org/1991/05/teaching-smart-people-how-to-learn.

22. F. A. Hayek, *The Road to Serfdom* (Chicago: University of Chicago Press, 2007), 70.

23. Daisy Grewal, "How Wealth Reduces Compassion: As Riches Grow, Empathy for Others Seems to Decline," *Scientific American*, April 10, 2012, https://www.scientificamerican.com/article/how-wealth-reduces-compassion/.

24. Arthur C. Brooks, *Love Your Enemies* (New York: Broadside Books, 2019), chap. 8.

25. J. R. Dempsey et al., "Program Management in Design and Development," in *Third Annual Aerospace Reliability and Maintainability Conference*, Society of Automotive Engineers, 1964, 7–8.

26. Danielle D. King, Ann Marie Ryan, and Linn Van Dyne, "Voice Resilience: Fostering Future Voice after Non-endorsement of Suggestions," *Journal of Occupational and Organizational Psychology* 92 no. 3 (September 2019): 535–565, available at https://onlinelibrary.wiley.com/doi/full/10.1111/joop.12275.

Conclusion: Avoiding Paternalism and Exploitation

1. Elisabeth Noelle-Neumann, "The Spiral of Silence: A Theory of Public Opinion," *Journal of Communication* 24, no. 2 (June 1974): 43–51.

2. Gerald Dworkin, "Paternalism," in *Stanford Encyclopedia of Philosophy*, 2017, accessed January 5, 2019, https://plato.stanford.edu/entries/paternalism/.

3. See Edward L. Deci and Richard M. Ryan, *Intrinsic Motivation and Self-Determination in Human Behavior* (New York: Plenum Press, 1885).

4. "How Many Nonprofit Colleges and Universities Have Closed Since 2016?" *EducationDive*, accessed June 17, 2019, https://www.educationdive.com/news/tracker-college-and-university-closings-and-consolidation/539961/.

5. Milton Friedman, "The Social Responsibility of Business to Increase Its Profits," *New York Times Magazine*, September 13, 1970, http://umich.edu/~thecore/doc/Friedman.pdf?mod=article inline.

6. Alexander Solzhenitsyn, *The Gulag Archipelago* (New York: Harper & Row, 1973), 24.

7. Christine Porath and Christine Pearson, "The Price of Incivility," *Harvard Business Review*, January-February 2013, https://hbr.org/2013/01/the-price-of-incivility.

8. Terry Warner, *Socialization, Self-Deception, and Freedom through Faith* (Provo, UT: Brigham Young University Press, 1973), 2.

9. Carol S. Dweck, *Mindset: The New Psychology of Success* (New York: Random House, 2006), 117.

10. Don Henley and Glenn Frey, "Hotel California," 1977.

11. Adam Nossiter, "35 Employees Committed Suicide. Will Their Bosses Go to Jail? *New York Times*, July 9, 2019, https://www.nytimes.com/2019/07/09/world/europe/france-telecom-trial.html.

12. Robert Waldinger, "What Makes a Good Life? Lessons from the Longest Study on Happiness," *TED*, uploaded January 25, 2016, video, 12:46, https://www.youtube.com/watch?v=8KkKuTCFvzI.

13. Harry McCraken, "Satya Nadella Rewrites Microsoft's Code," *Fast Company*, September 8, 2017, https://www.fastcompany.com/40457458/satya-nadella-rewrites-microsofts-code.

14. Acts 10:28, *Holy Bible, King James Version.*

Acknowledgments

I gratefully acknowledge the influence of leaders who create high levels of psychological safety, empowering others to perform beyond their expectations. I pay special tribute to my wife, Tracey, who exemplifies inclusion and practices unfeigned love toward all human beings. She is a living example of one who has mastered the art of creating and maintaining psychological safety. She has made our home a sanctuary of belonging for me and our children.

I'm grateful to Neal Maillet, the editorial director at Berrett-Koehler, and his team for creating psychological safety throughout the process of producing this book. He applies a combination of creative abrasion and genuine personal concern that motivates me to give my very best efforts. I also thank the entire Berrett-Koehler team and appreciate the distinctive culture of collaboration they have created for me as an author. I'm thankful for the talent and skill of Karen Seriguchi (copyediting), Leigh McLellan (design and composition), and Travis Wu (cover design). Finally, I thank my children for teaching me that my role is to create and preserve psychological safety in every relationship.

Index

A

accountability, levels of, 75–77
Adams, Abigail, 32
Adams, John, 31, 32
Ahn Chung Si, 24
Alexander the Great, 139
Alibaba, 130
Anderson, Brad, 12
Angelou, Maya, xv
AOL, 12
apprehension, 77
approval, seeking, 131–33
Arendt, Hannah, xvi
Aristotle, 31, 81–82
Atari, 12

B

Bennis, Warren, 2
bias, overcoming, 37–39
Blockbuster, 11, 107
blue zone, 77–82
Borders, 12
boundaries, creating, 134–35
Branden, Nathaniel, 37
Brigham Young University, 27, 56, 57
Bronkhorst, Babette, 54

C

Camus, Albert, 9
candor-for-cover concept, 100–102, 116
Caterpillar, 69–70
challenger safety
  creating, 99–102, 120–21
  importance of, 13–14
  innovation and, 12–14
  lack of, 11–12, 100–101, 104–5, 111–12
  leaders and, 116–19
  offensive innovation and, 69
  permission and, 103
  respect and, 102–3
  ridicule and, 115–16
  social exchange and, 103
  summary of, 11–13
  transitioning to, 98–99
Challenger space shuttle disaster, 13

change, organizational, 97–98
charisma, effects of, 82
Chinese Exclusion Act of 1882, 33
Christensen, C. Roland, 48
Circuit City, 12
cognition, 77
Compaq, 12
Confucianism, 25
contributor safety
  accountability and, 75–77
  blue zone and red zone for, 77–82
  defensive innovation and, 69, 70
  desire for, 66–67
  discretionary effort and, 78, 80
  as earned privilege, 66, 84
  emotional preparation for creating, 82–84
  lack of, 10, 66, 67
  performance and, 66–68, 71–72
  permission and, 71
  personality for creating, 81–82
  respect and, 71
  social exchange and, 71
  summary of, 10
  thinking beyond roles and, 88–90
  transitioning to, 73–75
creativity, 11, 99, 108
Csikszentmihalyi, Mihaly, 115–16
cultural differences, misunderstandings arising from, 1–2
curiosity, 54

D

dissent, 90, 119–20
diversity
  embracing, 37
  on teams, 114
  value of, 16
Drucker, Peter, 60, 114
Dweck, Carol, 34, 57
Dyson, James, 114

E

Edmondson, Amy, 2
elitism. *See* superiority, theories of
El Rancho Farms, 78
Emancipation Proclamation, 33
emotions
  contributor safety and, 82–84
  definition of, 77
  learner safety and, 52–55
ethnocentrism, 27
exclusion
  historical examples of, 33
  origins of, xvii, 34–35
execution
  definition of, 68
  innovation vs., 68
expectations, influence of, 49

exploitation, 15, 126–27, 130–31, 133

F

Facebook, 109
failure
  disconnecting fear from, 47–51
  as progress, 50
Fair Labor Standards Act of 1938, 33
families
  emotionally unsafe, 43–44
  inclusion safety in, 35–36
Farr-Wharton, Ben, 100
fear
  blue zone and, 79–80
  disconnecting from mistakes and failure, 47–51
  leadership and, xii–xiii
  learner safety and, 42–44
  stress and, 106–7
fellowship, false, 131–35
Florida, Richard, 59
France Télécom, 136
Francis, John, 52, 53
Fromm, Eric, 3

G

Gandhi, Mahatma, 19
Gates, Bill, 54
General Electric, 58
Geneva Steel, ix–xiii, 31, 69–70, 112
Google, 4

H

happiness, 136
Hitler, Adolf, 30
Hobbes, Thomas, xvii
Hochschild, Arlie Russell, 4
Hughes, Langston, xv
Huston, Boom, 78–80
Huston, Joe, 78

I

Immigration Act of 1965, 33
inclusion safety. *See also* exclusion
  in childhood, 20–21
  concept of, 20
  creation of, 8
  examples of, 24–25, 27–29
  in families, 35–36
  fragile nature of, 29
  importance of, 8
  lack of, 7–8
  learner safety and, 45
  overcoming bias and, 37–39
  permission and, 23
  qualifying for, 23, 26
  respect and, 23
  revoking, 29, 35
  self-regard and, 37

social exchange and, 23
summary of, 6–8
superiority and, 30–32
withholding, 22, 23, 26, 35
worth and, 21–22
Indian Removal Act of 1830, 33
innovation
assigning dissent and, 119–20
challenger safety and, 12–14, 100–101
collaboration and, 113
connectivity and, 97, 108, 114–15
definition of, 68
differences and, 114–15
execution vs., 68
importance of, 12
inquiry and, 109–11
interdisciplinary nature of, 112–13
offensive vs. defensive, 68–70
process of, 109
scaling, 13
social origins of, 107–8
stress and, 106–7
threshold, 98–99
types of, 108
inquiry, role of, 109–11

J

James, William, 7
Jim Crow laws, 33
Jobs, Steve, 108

K

Kafka, Franz, 37
Kahn, William, 2
Kahneman, Daniel, 48
Kasparov, Gary, 13
Kerr, Steve, 58
Kets de Vries, Manfred, 118
King, Martin Luther, Jr., 21, 95
knowledge workers, 58, 60
Knowles, Malcolm, 60
Kodak, 11
Krishnamurti, Jiddu, 41

L

leaders
challenger safety and, 116–19
as consumers vs. contributors, 15
demand for new, 137–39
dissent and, 90
fear and, xii–xiii
learner safety and, 60–61
listening by, 86–88
observation and, 84–85
roles of, 85
tell-to-ask ratio of, 85–86
learner safety
curiosity and, 54
emotions and, 52–55
examples of, 47–51, 52, 55–58
fear and, 42–44, 47–51
granting, 45–46, 52–54
importance of, 61–62

inclusion safety and, 45
lack of, 8–9
leaders and, 60–61
need for, 53, 55
in organizations, 58–62
permission and, 45
respect and, 45
in schools, 42–44, 47–51
social exchange and, 45, 57
summary of, 8–10
technology and, 53–54, 59–60
Lincoln, Abraham, 21, 33, 81
LinkedIn, 11
listening, 86–88
Lone Peak High School, 47
Luck, Kenny, 21

M

Ma, Jack, 130
Ma, Yo-Yo, 117
Madison, James, 130
Maslow, Abraham, 2, 106
McGregor, Douglas, 2
Mill, John Stuart, 80
Mills, C. Wright, xi
Morrison, Toni, 125
motivation, 77
Munoz, Oscar, 117

N

Nadella, Satya, 138
NASA, 13, 119
nativism, 27
Naturalization Act of 1790, 33
Netflix, 107
Niebuhr, Reinhold, 21
Nielsen, Barbara, 56

O

observation, 84–85
organization, definition of, 60
Orwell, George, 30
Otsuki, Tadao, 105

P

Palm, 12
paternalism, 14–15, 126–30
Pearson, Christine, 131
performance
components of, 68–70
contributor safety and, 66–68, 71–72
teams and, 67–68
transitioning from preparation to, 73–75
permission
challenger safety and, 103
contributor safety and, 71
definition of, 5
exploitation and, 15
inclusion safety and, 23
learner safety and, 45
paternalism and, 14, 126
respect and, 5–6
Porath, Christine, 131

psychological safety. *See also* challenger safety; contributor safety; inclusion safety; learner safety
- concept of, xiv, 2
- creation of, 16, 135
- hierarchy of needs and, 2, 3
- high level of, 5, 6
- lack of, xii, 4, 5, 14, 135
- leaders and, 137–39
- moral foundation of, 135–36
- nonbinary nature of, 4
- other terms for, 2
- research on, 2
- stages of, xiii, 6

Q

questions, asking, 110–11

R

racism, 32–33
Radio Shack, 12
Rawls, John, 26
red zone, 77–82
respect
- challenger safety and, 102–3
- contributor safety and, 71
- definition of, 5
- exploitation and, 15, 126
- inclusion safety and, 23
- learner safety and, 45
- paternalism and, 14
- permission and, 5–6

ridicule, reducing risk of, 115–16
Rogers, Carl, 2
roles
- learning specific, 88
- thinking beyond, 88–90

Roosevelt, Franklin D., 33

S

Salk, Jonas, 65
Schein, Edgar, 2, 29
schools
- failing, 42–44
- learner safety in, 42–44, 47–51

self-censoring instinct, 11, 43–44, 55, 99, 138
Seoul National University, 24
Sikahema, Vai, 55–58
silence, as indicator, 43
Simon, Herbert, 2
Simpson, Ace, 100
Smith, Craig B., 47–51, 118
Solzhenitsyn, Alexander, 131
Steele, Claude, 49
stereotype threat theory, 49
superiority, theories of, 30–32
Swanson, Celia, 5

T

Taylor, Frederick Winslow, 58
teams
- diverse, 114
- neuroplasticity of, 96–98
- performance and, 67–68

tell-to-ask continuum, 85–86
Thoreau, Henry David, 12
tiger teams, 119
Toys "R" Us, 12
trust
  family and, 35–36
  importance of, 34

U
University of Utah, 52
US Constitution, 32–33

V
volition, 77
von Hayek, Friedrich August, 118–19

W
Waldinger, Robert, 136
Warner, Terry, 132
Washington, George, 81
Welch, Jack, 58
white hackers, 119
Williams, Rowan, xvii
Wilson, Brian, 109
Wilson, Edward O., 99
women, discrimination against, 33, 34
worth vs. worthiness, 21–22, 29

Y
Yeats, W. B., xviii

Z
Zuckerberg, Mark, 109

About the Author

Timothy R. Clark is the founder and CEO of LeaderFactor, a global leadership consulting, training, and assessment organization. He is the author of five books and the developer of the EQometer™ emotional intelligence assessment. He earned a PhD from Oxford University in social science.

The 4 Stages of Psychological Safety Behavioral Guide

If you would like additional guidance for creating psychological safety in your organization, feel free to download "The 4 Stages of Psychological Safety Behavioral Guide" at

https://www.LeaderFactor.com/PsychologicalSafetyGuide

The 4 Stages of Psychological Safety Assessment & Training for Teams

If your team would like to accelerate the process of developing psychological safety, please visit

https://www.LeaderFactor.com/PsychologicalSafety

to learn about our team assessment and training solutions.

Also by Timothy R. Clark

Leading with Character and Competence

Moving Beyond Title, Position, and Authority

Three-time CEO, Oxford-trained scholar, and consultant Timothy R. Clark shows how greatness emerges from a powerful combination of character and competence. Character is the core; competence is the crust. Both are essential: character is the foundation that competence must be built on. "Those of good character who lack competence remain ineffective. But competent leaders who lack character become dangerous. Clark spotlights the four most important components of character and competence and offers a series of eloquent, inspiring, and actionable reflections on what's needed to build each one.

Paperback, 192 pages, ISBN 978-1-5230-8768-6
PDF ebook, ISBN 978-1-5230-8769-3
ePub ebook ,ISBN 978-1-5230-8770-9
Digital audio, ISBN 978-1-5230-8771-6

800.929.2929

Berrett–Koehler
Publishers

Berrett-Koehler is an independent publisher dedicated to an ambitious mission: *Connecting people and ideas to create a world that works for all.*

Our publications span many formats, including print, digital, audio, and video. We also offer online resources, training, and gatherings. And we will continue expanding our products and services to advance our mission.

We believe that the solutions to the world's problems will come from all of us, working at all levels: in our society, in our organizations, and in our own lives. Our publications and resources offer pathways to creating a more just, equitable, and sustainable society. They help people make their organizations more humane, democratic, diverse, and effective (and we don't think there's any contradiction there). And they guide people in creating positive change in their own lives and aligning their personal practices with their aspirations for a better world.

And we strive to practice what we preach through what we call "The BK Way." At the core of this approach is *stewardship,* a deep sense of responsibility to administer the company for the benefit of all of our stakeholder groups, including authors, customers, employees, investors, service providers, sales partners, and the communities and environment around us. Everything we do is built around stewardship and our other core values of *quality, partnership, inclusion,* and *sustainability.*

This is why Berrett-Koehler is the first book publishing company to be both a B Corporation (a rigorous certification) and a benefit corporation (a for-profit legal status), which together require us to adhere to the highest standards for corporate, social, and environmental performance. And it is why we have instituted many pioneering practices (which you can learn about at www.bkconnection.com), including the Berrett-Koehler Constitution, the Bill of Rights and Responsibilities for BK Authors, and our unique Author Days.

We are grateful to our readers, authors, and other friends who are supporting our mission. We ask you to share with us examples of how BK publications and resources are making a difference in your lives, organizations, and communities at www.bkconnection.com/impact.

Dear reader,

Thank you for picking up this book and welcome to the worldwide BK community! You're joining a special group of people who have come together to create positive change in their lives, organizations, and communities.

What's BK all about?

Our mission is to connect people and ideas to create a world that works for all.

Why? Our communities, organizations, and lives get bogged down by old paradigms of self-interest, exclusion, hierarchy, and privilege. But we believe that can change. That's why we seek the leading experts on these challenges—and share their actionable ideas with you.

A welcome gift

To help you get started, we'd like to offer you a **free copy** of one of our bestselling ebooks:

www.bkconnection.com/welcome

When you claim your **free ebook**, you'll also be subscribed to our blog.

Our freshest insights

Access the best new tools and ideas for leaders at all levels on our blog at ideas.bkconnection.com.

Sincerely,

Your friends at Berrett-Koehler